A Borderlands Town in Transition

A Borderlands Town
in Transition

LAREDO, 1755–1870

By
Gilberto Miguel
Hinojosa

Texas A&M University Press

COLLEGE STATION

Library of Congress Cataloging in Publication Data

Hinojosa, Gilberto Miguel, 1942–
    A borderlands town in transition.

    Bibliography: p.
    Includes index.
        1. Laredo (Tex.)—History.   2. Laredo (Tex.)—
    Social conditions.   3. Laredo (Tex.)—Economic con-
    ditions.   4. Mexican Americans—Texas—Laredo—
    History.   I. Title.
    F394.L2H56   1983   976.4′462   83-45096
    ISBN 0-89096-160-3 (cloth)
    ISBN 0-89096-977-9 (pbk.)

Manufactured in the United States of America
First Paperback Edition

A mis padres, José H. Hinojosa y
Concepción González de Hinojosa,
a mi esposa, Gloria, y a mis hijas,
María del Carmen y Teresita

Contents

Illustrations

Preface

Rapid transcontinental expansion by the United States during the nineteenth century obscured the presence of earlier Indian and Spanish settlement in the Southwest, but the heritage of these peoples survived and, in time, was rediscovered. Disregard for the history of these earlier settlements stemmed from the struggle for control of the continent. As a result of the Mexican War and the annexation of Texas, the United States subjugated the people of the Southwest during the 1840s. Overpowering American economic and political forces dismantled large parts of the older Hispanic institutions and economic structures soon after the conquest. The past seemed to disappear, but Spain's centuries-long roots in the Southwest could not be completely pried loose, and some sought to nurture them and recapture the past's Hispanic grandeur and significance.

The groundwork for the rediscovery of the Hispanic history of the Southwest was laid in California in the nineteenth century by Hubert Howe Bancroft. His writings called attention to the historical role of the Indian and the Spanish-Mexican in western North America. Among Bancroft's many successors, Herbert E. Bolton led the way in uncovering valuable archival materials, defining the extent for the borderlands region, studying the principal institutions of the Spanish empire, editing historical documents for the Southwest, and stressing the comparative study of the history of the Americas. Prominent among the many historians who built on the foundations laid by Bancroft and Bolton were Texas scholars Charles W. Hackett and Carlos E. Castañeda.[1]

[1] For an evaluation of the work of Hubert Howe Bancroft see John W. Caughey, *Hubert Howe Bancroft, Historian of the West*; and Donald Cutter, "Dedication to the Memory of Hubert Howe Bancroft," *Arizona and the West* 2 (Summer, 1960): 105–106. For a brief evaluation of the writings of Herbert E. Bolton, see John Francis Bannon,

Focusing on Spanish political, ecclesiastical, and military history, most studies of the borderlands have concentrated on missions, *presidios* (garrisons), and *cabildos* (town councils) as vehicles of Spanish culture and imperial power. Because historical records are largely bureaucratic documents, existing scholarly works present, quite understandably, the picture of a society dominated by institutions. The importance of the military, religious orders, and *cabildos* is unquestionable, since the objectives of these institutions embodied Spanish expectations in the area. But with few exceptions, the details as to how people lived out these expectations or changed them to meet the exigencies of frontier life have been left out of scholarly works. Studies of the economics of land, labor, and trade describe other facets of Spanish settlement in the Southwest without casting more than an occasional glance at the society in which institutions and economic forces operated. At best these studies describe the relationship between certain groups—government and ecclesiastical elites, Indians, soldiers, and traders—and institutions.[2]

Recently, however, the influence of other disciplines on history has offered scholars new methods and perspectives for investigating neglected aspects of southwestern history.[3] An-

---

Bolton and the Spanish Borderlands, pp. 3–19; Charles W. Hackett, *Pichardo's Treatise on the Limits of Louisiana and Texas*; and Carlos E. Castañeda, *Our Catholic Heritage in Texas.*

[2] Donald E. Worcester, "The Significance of the Spanish Borderlands to the United States," *Western Historical Quarterly* 7 (January, 1976): 5–18. Although somewhat dated, the bibliographical essay in John Francis Bannon, *The Spanish Borderlands Frontier, 1513–1821*, pp. 257–87, remains valuable. A major work on social history is Paul Horgan, *Great River: The Rio Grande in North American History.* Horgan's historical methodology has received considerable criticism from scholars, and these flaws have unfortunately prevented the acceptance of the subtle cultural tones sketched by Horgan. See Frank D. Reeve, "A Letter to Clio," *New Mexico Historical Review* 31 (April, 1956): 102–32.

[3] Anthropologist Edward H. Spicer, in *Cycles of Conquest*, and *Plural Society in the Southwest*, describes the relationships between the Indians of the borderlands and their Spanish, Mexican, and American conquerors. D. W. Meinig's *Southwest: Three Peoples in Geographical Change* is a study of the Southwest by a demographic geographer. Sociologist Frances Leon Swadesh, in *Los Primeros Pobladores: Hispanic Americans of the Ute Frontier*, analyzes the historical basis for the social structure in New Mexico's Chama Valley.

thropologists have described formal and informal relationships between Indians and their various conquerors, and sociologists have researched the foundations of present social structures. Some historians of the American frontier, employing quantitative techniques used by sociologists, have directed their attention to population movements, occupational mobility, property ownership, marriage and family patterns, dwelling and household structure, and other demographic characteristics of the West.[4] Their influence is evident in recent demographic research on the borderlands. Most of this work concentrates on the post-1848 period, for which data and sources in English are readily available in the United States. Studies on Mexican Americans in California are among the several worthwhile contributions in this area.[5] Only a few works cover the Spanish-Mexican borderlands, and these are mostly regional or provincial in scope.[6]

[4]Ground was broken in Western history by Merle E. Curti's *The Making of an American Community: A Case Study of Democracy in a Frontier County*. A more recent work, James Edward Davis's *Frontier America, 1800–1840: A Comparative Analysis of the Settlement Process* provides an excellent description of the demography of the westward movement.

[5]Richard Griswald del Castillo, *The Los Angeles Barrio, 1850–1890: A Social History*; Albert Michael Camarillo, *Chicanos in a Changing Society: From Mexican Pueblos to American Barrios in Santa Barbara and Southern California, 1848–1930*. Perhaps the best bibliographical essay on Chicano history is found in Juan Gómez-Quiñones and Luis Leobardo Arroyo, "On the State of Chicano History: Observations on Its Development, Interpretations and Theory, 1970–1974," *Western Historical Quarterly* 7 (April, 1976): 155–85. Among the works pertinent to this study and not included in their otherwise extensive list are David Thomas Bailey, "Stratification and Ethnic Differentiation in Santa Fe, 1860 and 1870" (Ph.D. diss., University of Texas at Austin, 1975), and James M. McReynolds, "Family Life in a Borderlands Community: Nacogdoches, Texas, 1779–1861" (Ph.D. diss., Texas Tech University, 1978).

[6]A recent study which incorporates demographic material is by Oakah L. Jones, Jr., *Los Paisanos: Spanish Settlers on the Northern Frontier of New Spain*. Other interesting demographic studies of the borderlands area are those of Alicia V. Tjarks, "Comparative Demographic Analysis of Texas, 1777–1793," *Southwestern Historical Quarterly* 77 (January, 1974): 291–338, and "Demographic, Ethnic, and Occupational Structures of New Mexico, 1790," *The Americas* 35 (July, 1978): 45–88; and Andrew A. Tijerina, "*Tejanos* and Texas: Native *Mexicanos* of Texas, 1820–1850" (Ph.D. diss., University of Texas at Austin, 1977). Both authors analyze communities over time, but both are interested more in the development of the province than that of any one town. Henry F. Dobyn's *Spanish Colonial Tucson: A Demographic History*, provides new insights into the role of the mission and the *presidio* in Indian-Spanish relations.

This study of Laredo between 1755 and 1870 also addresses demographic topics, focusing on the dynamics of population change within the community. Laredo's relative smallness made it possible to study the entire community, a procedure which enabled me to trace individuals from one census to another. Laredo's existence since the mid-1700s provided an opportunity to describe and analyze the adjustment made by the townspeople to several sovereignties: Spanish, Mexican, American, Confederate, and American again.

Concerned mostly with military and political events related to these transitions and with genealogical interests, Laredo historians have overlooked the data that reveal the effects of public events on the townspeople. Their studies leave unanswered many important questions pertaining to demographic change in the town.[7] What were the rates of population growth and decline? What brought about the population changes, and how did the fluctuations affect Laredoans? Were the townspeople a homogeneous group or a community exhibiting divisions based on time of arrival, race, wealth, politics, or ethnic background? Was there a source of unity among Laredoans and, if so, was this

[7] Shortly after the American conquest, the issue of land ownership arose, and the records of the allotment of lands were retrieved from the town's archives. Not until the 1930s and 1940s were documentary resources utilized in a historical manner. The archives from the Spanish, Mexican, and early American periods were saved from destruction by Seb S. Wilcox, a court reporter with an interest in Laredo's past. He and Florencio Andrés, pastor of St. Augustine church, spent countless hours arranging, annotating, and translating documents. Later they assisted the Works Progress Administration in the transcription of most of the records. Father Andrés added notes to entries in the church records. Wilcox published three articles, "Laredo During the Texas Republic," "The Laredo City Elections and the Riot of 1886," and "The Spanish Archives of Laredo" in the *Southwestern Historical Quarterly* 42 (October, 1938): 83–107, 45 (July, 1941): 1–23, and 49 (January, 1946): 341–60, respectively. He also occasionally wrote letters and sent research notes to the editor of the *Quarterly*.

Andrés's and Wilcox's work laid the foundation for other Laredo historians: Rogelia O. García, *Laredo, Dolores, Revilla: Three Sister Settlements*, and *The Song of La Grande Agua*; Jerry Don Thompson, *Sabers on the Rio Grande*, and *Vaqueros in Blue and Grey*; and J. B. Wilkinson, *Laredo and the Rio Grande Frontier*. Another important work on Laredo is John Dennis Riley's "Santos Benavides: His Influence on the Lower Rio Grande 1823–1891" (Ph.D. diss., Texas Christian University, 1976). James Arthur Irby's "Line on the Rio Grande: War and Trade on the Confederate Frontier, 1861–1865" (Ph.D. diss., University of Georgia, 1969) also makes extensive reference to events in Laredo.

unity threatened or destroyed at any time? Was Laredo self-sufficient or was it dependent upon external sources for its security, its economic well-being, and its sense of purpose?

A demographic study of Laredo in the prerailroad years may explain in part the present-day political and economic prominence of Mexican Americans there. Since it had been hardened by transitions experienced before the 1870s, Laredoans were able to maintain in its basic outline the social structure planted in the Spanish period. Laredo's development in the early period also commands attention because its population in the Spanish and Mexican periods was not significantly smaller than the population of Santa Fe, San Antonio, and Los Angeles. In fact, in these periods Laredo had a larger population than La Bahía del Espíritu Santo and Nacogdoches in Texas, Albuquerque in Nuevo México, and Santa Bárbara in California. There were many other towns smaller than Laredo. Many of these passed into oblivion. Laredo was spared their fate because its geographical location placed it at an economic crossroads. Thus the historical experience of Laredoans may be representative of that lived by settlers and sojourners in both small and large communities in the chaparral region and across the borderlands.

The findings from this study of Laredo may also shed new light on the history of the Southwest. Many historians of the borderlands tend to assume that communities on the northern Spanish-Mexican frontier were somewhat static and that daily life was governed in almost every detail by royal decree. Because institutions in the borderlands were designed to carry out imperial objectives of expansion and defense, many studies give the impression that these communities either had no goals of their own or were not allowed to pursue them.[8] This book shows that Laredoans acted primarily out of concern for their own best interests and only secondarily, if at all, to advance imperial or national goals. Further study of other communities may prove Laredo's experience was common to other borderlands towns,

[8] This interpretation of a static Spanish-Mexican society is at times employed to stress the aggressive nature of the Anglo-American westward movement. See Bannon, *The Spanish Borderlands Frontier*, pp. 5–7, and Seymour V. Connor, *Texas: A History*, p. 54.

but if the evidence suggests otherwise, this investigation at least
will have raised the questions.

Most primary sources for Laredo's history during the Spanish and Mexican periods are found in the Laredo Archives
housed at St. Mary's University of San Antonio. For the American era the Laredo city records, Webb County records, some
records of the State of Texas, and the manuscript returns of the
United States censuses of 1850, 1860, 1870, and 1880 are the
principal sources. The Laredo Archives contain a number of decrees, censuses, wills, military and municipal reports to higher
authorities, and some trial records. These materials have been
examined by a handful of historians interested in Laredo, but
until now none has investigated and analyzed them thoroughly
or with the intention of studying the demographic history of
Laredo.[9] Very little has heretofore been written about Laredo
from city and county records, and the census returns have not
been utilized at all. Materials for military activities on the Rio
Grande can be found in the Texas State Archives and in the Barker Texas History Center at the University of Texas at Austin.
(Detailed statistical data, based on these sources, are in the appendix to this book.)

[9] As with all historical records, critical judgment must be employed in the use of
the materials in the Laredo Archives. For example, reports of Indian threats seem at
times exaggerated. Occasionally the accuracy of a census is questionable, such as the
census of 1833, which is uncannily similar to that of 1831. For the most part, however,
there is little reason to doubt the validity of census tabulations, reports made to the governor, descriptions of the settlement, and the recounting of events.

Acknowledgments

THE preparation for this book began with my graduate training at the University of Texas at Austin, and I am indebted to all my professors there, particularly Dr. John E. Sunder and Dr. Barnes F. Lathrop, who worked long hours with me, carefully examining my work and offering invaluable suggestions. I also wish to thank Dr. Nettie Lee Benson, Dr. Américo Paredes, Dr. Norman D. Brown, and Dr. L. Tuffly Ellis for their time and guidance. Omissions or errors that may appear in this book persist despite their advice to the contrary.

I am grateful for the research support provided by the Center for Mexican American Studies and the Department of History of the University of Texas at Austin and for the photographs furnished by the Institute of Texan Cultures in San Antonio. In the process of preparing this work I also incurred debts to Carmen Perry, archivist at St. Mary's University of San Antonio, who arranged the Laredo Archives and made them accessible to me and other scholars; to Dr. Thomas C. Greaves, director of the Division of Social Studies, and my other colleagues at the University of Texas at San Antonio for encouraging me in my project; to Luciano Guajardo, director of the Laredo Public Library, for directing me to a variety of resources and providing some of the photographs; to the Reverend Kenneth Hennessy, pastor of St. Augustine Catholic Church in Laredo, who allowed me to use parish records; to Laredo and Webb County officials who assisted me in finding documents; and in a special way to Dr. José Roberto Juárez and the Laredo Council for the Arts, without whose enthusiastic and generous backing the manuscript could not have been published.

Whatever pride I can take in this my first book I must share with my family, to whom I dedicate it, and with my professors and friends who helped me to complete it; whatever remuneration I receive I would like to share with the people of Laredo by assigning the royalties to the Webb County Historical Commission.

A Borderlands Town in Transition

CHAPTER 1

Implantation, Growth, and Maturity, 1755–1810

M ORE than two hundred years after the conquest of Tenochtitlan vast areas in northeastern New Spain remained unsettled. Explorers of the sixteenth and seventeenth centuries judged these lands infertile and the natives uncooperative. Settlers chose to colonize the rich valleys of the upper Rio Grandè and the mining districts of Nuevo León and Coahuila. To prevent a possible French expansion into these areas, *conquistadores* ventured far to the east and planted the Spanish banner near the Louisiana border. Hidden inside this arch of settlement reaching from Nuevo León to Louisiana, skirted by the string of missions, forts, and villages that maintained the supply lines to the distant outposts, El Seno Mexicano (the Mexican Gulf Coast) remained a desolate barren plain until the mid-eighteenth century.

Bounded on the west by the Sierra Madre Oriental, El Seno Mexicano extended north from the Pánuco along the Gulf Coast to the Provinces of Nuevo León, Coahuila, and Texas, which it resembled physiographically. It was hot and dry, and appeared uninhabitable. Prospective settlers could farm only the bottomlands of the few streams that crossed this chaparral desert. Yet the land provided sufficient vegetation for wild cattle and mustangs and for the livestock that any settler would bring. Undesirable as El Seno Mexicano appeared initially, by the early 1700s it offered new opportunities for survival and wealth to *rancheros* and settlers from the adjoining areas, where growing herds had created a need for new grazing lands.[1]

Along with possibilities for expansion, however, the area

[1] Fray Vicente Santa María, "Relación histórica de la colonia de Nuevo Santander y costa del seno mexicano," in *Estado general de las fundaciones hechas por d. José de Escandón en la Colonia de Nuevo Santander*, II, 35–36, 360–64.

presented many dangers to settlers. In the southern portion, Janambres, Napanames, Aracales, and other tribes that had been pushed into the rugged Tamaulipa ranges—the Sierra Gorda—periodically sallied from their mountain refuges in attempts to retake their lands or simply to survive. Farther north, the same Apaches, Lipans, and Comanches who made incursions into Coahuila and Nuevo León also swept down into El Seno Mexicano.[2] Threatening and yet promising, this semiarid plain could be settled only by a strong, deliberate, and carefully prepared colonizing expedition.

The Colonization of Nuevo Santander

The man selected for this task was José de Escandón, a peninsular who had successfully pursued a military career in New Spain, married well, and held a position of prominence in Querétaro. Escandón's experience and social status made him a likely choice first to pacify the southern region and later to lead the colonization projects. In 1746 Escandón, by then Conde de la Sierra Gorda, received the appointment as *conquistador*, captain general, and governor of the area recently named the Province of Nuevo Santander. In this capacity he planned and organized a several-pronged *entrada* which resulted in the establishment of twenty towns and eighteen missions between 1749 and 1755. With the foundation of Laredo, the last of these towns, Escandón's colonization project was considered complete.[3]

The settlement of El Seno Mexicano differed significantly from earlier colonization enterprises in the borderlands. In the *entradas* of Juan de Oñate into New Mexico in 1598, Luis de Carvajal into Nuevo León in 1659, and Alonso de León and Fray Damián de Massanet into Texas in 1686 and 1689, the attraction of great wealth or a foreign threat called for conquest far beyond the line of settlement. The special objective and the bypassing of large unsettled areas made these early *entradas* appear force-

[2] David M. Vigness, trans. and ed., "Nuevo Santander in 1795: A Provincial Inspection by Félix Calleja," *Southwestern Historical Quarterly* 75 (April, 1972): 464.

[3] Lawrence F. Hill, *José de Escandón and the Founding of Nuevo Santander: A Study of Spanish Colonization*, pp. 5, 19–21, 56–58.

ful and dramatic in comparison with the gradual expansion later into Nuevo Santander. Yet both patterns were in keeping with Spanish tradition.[4]

Slow, well-plotted incorporation of areas from adjacent provinces was the result of steady population growth and the consequent need for new sources of wealth. To facilitate this colonization, men of stature from well-established interior regions, such as José de Escandón from Querétaro, received authority from the Crown and made the necessary investments. The mid-level leadership and settlers came from nearby provinces. Later, growth within a colony followed a scaled-down version of this same expansion-settlement-expansion process. Through this pattern of gradualism Laredo was established.[5]

In the northeastern corner of the new province of Nuevo Santander, Escandón planted settlements along the Rio Grande as defense outposts against the *indios bárbaros* (nomadic Indians). He brought colonists from Nuevo León to Mier and Camargo in 1749 and the following year he recruited *rancheros* from Coahuila to settle upriver in Revilla and Dolores. Notwithstanding dangers and difficulties in the high brush country, these towns prospered, and five years later there was need for expansion. Escandón agreed to the request for a new settlement, and colonists from Dolores and Revilla then moved to vacant lands upriver. They named the settlement San Agustín de Laredo.[6]

The Founding of Laredo

Located in the northern tip of Nuevo Santander, Laredo was an extension of Revilla and Dolores. Revilla's prosperity rivaled that of the other towns along the Rio Grande. Flanked by Mier and the Hacienda de Dolores and prevented from expanding

---

[4]Vito Alessio Robles, *Coahuila y Texas desde la consumación de la independencia hasta el tratado de Guadalupe Hidalgo*, pp. 19–20; Herbert Eugene Bolton, *The Spanish Borderlands: A Chronicle of Old Florida and the Southwest*, pp. 170–77, 207–31; Philip Wayne Powell, *Soldiers, Indians and Silver*, p. 2.

[5]See *Estado general de las fundaciones*, II, 115, 118, 121.

[6]Ibid., I, 429–30, 440.

southward by the prosperous town of Camargo, Revilla's growing population looked for new land above the Paso de Jacinto.
Perhaps intending to capitalize on these land and population
pressures, don José Vázquez Borrego, founder and head of the
hacienda (large feudal estate) of Dolores, seized the opportunity
of Escandón's visit to the Rio Grande to propose a colonization
project in northern Nuevo Santander. Vázquez Borrego nomi-
nated as leader one of his administrators, who later became his
son-in-law, don Tomás Sánchez de la Barreda y Gallardo.[7]

Originally from Nuevo León, don Tomás Sánchez had come
from Coahuila where he had managed another *hacienda*. His
family had been associated with different settlement expeditions
in those two provinces, a background and experience which
served him well on the Rio Grande frontier. Supported by Vázquez Borrego, Sánchez received from Escandón political and
military authority to carry out the new colonizing expedition. In
return for his investment Sánchez was promised land. Comply-
ing with Escandón's suggestion, Sánchez explored the Nueces
area, but opted not to settle there, perhaps because such an outpost would have been too removed from other settlements. Instead, on May 15, 1755, Sánchez brought three families to an
area between the Jacinto and Garza fords on the Rio Grande.[8]

With the establishment of Laredo, Escandón's mission was
accomplished, and the viceroy shortly thereafter commissioned
a *visita*, or inspection, of El Seno Mexicano. Such an inquiry
was part of the system of checks and balances within the Spanish
government. Crown appointees such as Escandón usually received wide discretionary authority over people and wealth.
These appointees were fully aware, however, that abuses and ir-
regularities could be reported to the *visitador* (inspector), who
evaluated their performance once their term of office or assignment was completed. As in other inspections, the selection of
the *visitador* and the rigor of the investigation were open to political pressures.[9] Escandón's rapid success in settling an area as

---

[7] J. B. Wilkinson, *Laredo and the Rio Grande Frontier*, pp. 24–26.

[8] Ben Cuellar Ximenes, *Gallant Outcasts*, p. 89; *Estado general de las fundaciones*, I, 444–45.

[9] C. H. Haring, *The Spanish Empire in America*, pp. 148–57; Charles Gibson,
Spain in America, p. 100.

vast as Nuevo Santander and his great profit from such an un-
promising venture gave rise to suspicion and jealousy. The *visita*
of El Seno Mexicano in 1757 may have been inspired by such
sentiments since the Conde, and later his son, subsequently
struggled through a lengthy legal process fighting charges stemming from the colonization of Nuevo Santander.[10]

Suspicions of Escandón's actions were absent in the actual
inquiry, however. The *visitador*, don José Tienda de Cuervo,
and his assistants reached the northern edge of the province by
mid-1757 and set about the task of describing the Rio Grande
settlements. They interviewed all the heads of households, ask-
ing them to list the members of their families and households,
the size of their herds, and the availability of weapons for defense. They reviewed the colonization process and also heard
complaints and suggestions. From the information gathered
they wrote their report.[11]

Their account reveals that the three settlements at the very
tip of Nuevo Santander varied in population size (Revilla, 557;
Dolores, 122; and Laredo, 85), but resembled each other very
closely in their social structure. In all three, most members of
the households were bound by nuclear family ties. Over half of
the family and household units were made up of five or fewer
members. In Revilla and Dolores over half of the families with
children reported three children or less; in Laredo the number
of children was only slightly higher. Even *solteros*, unmarried
related or unrelated adults, resided for the most part in households composed of families. In Revilla, such single adults made
up only a small fraction of the population because they tended to
migrate to Laredo. All three settlements thus displayed a social
structure based upon the family, with very few households
headed by single adults. The pattern was so common that the
visitadores and the settlers found it unnecessary to allude to it,
but family unity constituted a social reality that gave the community strength and purpose in the early years of settlement.

The main problem that surfaced from Tienda de Cuervo's
interviews was the question of the distribution of land. Escandón had decreed that the land granted to the towns be held in

[10]Wilkinson, *Laredo and the Rio Grande Frontier*, pp. 43–46.
[11]*Estado general de las fundaciones*, I, 5–10.

common in order to avoid petty disputes and land monopolies which would stave off immigration. Those interviewed stated that while this arrangement attracted immigrants it also created an uncertainty which discouraged land and housing improvements.[12] The *visitadores* concurred in this opinion and noted that this problem affected all the town settlements along the Rio Grande.

Besides being anxious to acquire title to the land in order to build and improve their holdings, these early settlers of Laredo were no doubt concerned also with securing positions of prominence in the town before other newcomers arrived. Within two years Laredo had grown from a handful of settlers to eighty-four people. The push of population from Revilla, as well as the attraction of open lands for the grazing of sheep and goats around Laredo, would soon encourage even more immigration to the new townsite. While this was indeed the purpose for the establishment of Laredo, *los primeros pobladores*, the town's founders, would have preferred that change not come so rapidly.

As things stood, Laredo was don Tomás Sánchez's *hacienda*, much as Dolores was Vázquez Borrego's feudal estate. Sánchez owned about three-fourths of all the horses, both tamed and on the range, one-fourth of the sheep, half of the cattle, and all of the mules and oxen in Laredo. Furthermore, when the social and economic predominance of the entire Sánchez family is examined, Laredo appears to have been their private acquisition rather than the public colonization project it was intended to be.[13]

Laredo was a small settlement—the engineer of the inspection party characterized it as a *rancho*—yet it retained a certain flexibility similar to that of Revilla, the nearest town on the Rio Grande.[14] In Laredo three heads of households listed servants,

---

[12] Ibid., I, 428–30, 432–36, 444–50.

[13] Ibid., II, 123–25, 449. For a description of the *hacienda* as an economic and social unit, see François Chevalier's *Land and Society in Colonial Mexico*, pp. 264, 277–80.

[14] The town, or *villa*, was a legal entity usually created by the commissioned leader of an expedition and juridically dependent on the governor (Haring, *Spanish Empire in America*, pp. 147–53). For the description of Laredo as a *rancho* see Herbert Eugene Bolton, "Tienda de Cuervo's *Ynspección* of Laredo, 1757," *Southwestern Historical Quarterly* 6 (January, 1903): 202.

and one householder in Revilla owned a slave. None of the heads of households in either settlement could boast, as did the *hacendado* (*hacienda* owner) of Dolores, of the twelve-man crew of servants who also doubled as *vaqueros* (cowhands) and private militiamen. Vázquez Borrego, the *hacendado*, quite naturally owned all the horses on the estate. In Revilla nine of the fifty-seven individuals listing tamed horses owned half of all the horses in town. Nevertheless, the median number of horses per owner was twelve. In Laredo two persons owned half of the horses, and the median number of horses per person was six. When the overall number of horses, mules, sheep, goats, cattle, and burros is considered on a per capita basis, Laredo resembled Revilla more than it did Dolores. Although in both Laredo and Revilla prosperity and control were concentrated in the hands of a few, these communities exhibited a considerable measure of economic and personal independence.[15]

Thus, at this early point in its development, Laredo found itself at a crossroads. Certain facets of its economic and social structure as well as perhaps the expectations of its *primeros pobladores* gave Laredo the appearance of an *hacienda*. Yet the structure of the community had sufficient flexibility to allow a good measure of opportunity and personal independence. In this it resembled a *villa*, or town. Had the government allotted lands at this point, Laredo might have evolved as an extension of Dolores. Instead, ten years elapsed before the partition of the lands. During that time the flow of Revillanos added diversity and division to Laredo, which prevented any one group from dominating the settlement. Yet through this period of maturation Laredo maintained stability based on family bonds. Progress and growth in the early years did not disrupt the family unit. Events and developments within the next few decades, however, would alter and threaten family cohesion and unity.

The Expansion of Laredo

Within a decade, at the time of a second *visita* in 1767, the population of Laredo had more than doubled, rising from 85 to 185.

---

[15] *Estado general de las fundaciones*, I, 428–50.

The *visitadores*, Juan Fernando de Palacios and José de Ossorio, acknowledged this growth and change of character in Laredo by conferring on the town the designation of *villa* and by allotting the lands. After setting aside the traditional town common, or *ejidos*, they assigned, with all proper ceremony, *porciones* (parcels) with river fronts and town lots to all heads of households according to seniority. By issuing titles to the land, they brought security to Laredo and set the foundation for the future wealth and position of the recipients.

At the time, however, the *visita* caused some problems for the well-established Sánchez interests. The royal commissioners awarded Sánchez and his family only seven of the sixty-five assigned *porciones*. Slightly over four-fifths of the *porciones* went to new settlers, many of whom were former *rancheros* from Revilla, farther down the river. Their need for new grazing land had encouraged a settlement on the west side of the river, opposite Laredo. The *visita* officially brought these *rancheros* under the jurisdiction of Laredo.[16]

The impact of this economic reorganization was felt the following year when the town landowners selected a new *cabildo*, or city council. The *alcalde* (mayor), his fellow aldermen, and the treasurer were all former Revillanos now residing opposite Laredo on the west bank. In order to display their newly acquired status and to improve the value of their properties, the new officials removed the town records to their side of the river and declared it the center of the townsite. Only the governor's intervention prevented the success of this scheme. The *alcalde* was removed, and Sánchez assumed the post, at least temporarily.[17]

The controversy between the *primeros pobladores* and the newcomers on the opposite bank was far from over. The more numerous recent arrivals continued to dominate the *cabildo* and occasionally recaptured the mayoralty. But Sánchez retained his

[16] Acta de la Visita de Laredo, 1767, General Land Office, Austin.

[17] *Estado general de las fundaciones*, II, 125, José Ossorio to Señores Capitán, Cabildo y Apoderados de Laredo, 8 April 1768, Juan Fernando Palacios to Joseph Martínez de Sotomayor, 30 August 1768, Laredo Archives, St. Mary's University of San Antonio. Also see decree of Vicente González de Santianes, 3 July 1770, Laredo Archives.

position of *capitán* of the local militia. The conflict of authority no doubt perpetuated the friction between the two groups. It also caused Sánchez considerable frustration, as is evident in the wild charges he made against a *regidor* (alderman) and other *rancheros* from the west bank. He accused Salvador González Ydalgo and his family of harassing and maltreating the stock of owners on the east side. The governor did not give the accusations much credence, and González Ydalgo remained in office.[18]

Factionalism flared again when Nicolás Campos Castellanos, the new treasurer, was charged with embezzling 119 pesos, 3 reales, from the town coffers. Sánchez promptly removed him from office and jailed him. When Campos Castellanos failed to restore the amount, Sánchez confiscated all of his property, which was sold at public auction, netting the town more than the amount embezzled. Later the governor exiled Campos Castellanos from Laredo. The former *alcalde*, José Martínez de Sotomayor, may have been negligent in his supervisory duties and thus partly responsible for the embezzlement. However, Sánchez apparently did not feel secure enough to measure out similar punishment to Martínez, a prominent *ranchero* from the west bank.[19]

West bank interests continued to challenge don Tomás's authority in other ways. The local priest, who had come from Revilla with the new settlers, served as their representative. On one occasion, he provided asylum to a drunk. He also extended sanctuary to Campos Castellanos. Later he snubbed the newly elected *cabildo* by not receiving Alcalde Sánchez and the aldermen at the church door at Sunday Mass.[20]

More impersonal decentralizing forces also eroded Sánchez's dominance. The general economic growth of the region

[18] Vicente González Santianes to Tomás Sánchez, 7 December 1770, Laredo Archives.

[19] Deposition of Nicolás Campos Castellanos, 15 April 1771, Nicolás Campos Castellanos to Vicente González Santianes, 13 June 1771, and Vicente González Santianes to Tomás Sánchez, 22 March 1771, all in Laredo Archives.

[20] Testimony of Joseph Leonardo Sánchez in the proceeding against Cayetano Peña, 10 October 1770, summary of accusations against Nicolás Campos Castellanos, 22 April 1771, and Vicente González Santianes to Tomás Sánchez, 1 March 1771, all in Laredo Archives.

brought a gradual expansion on the west bank and other areas away from the town. To stem this population movement away from Laredo, Sánchez used his position as *alcalde* and his influence with the governor to order back to Laredo those who had moved to the west bank and those who had followed their grazing cattle to the outlying rural areas. He issued *bandos* (proclamations, decrees) directed at the general public and at specific individuals, threatening them with fines and jail terms if they did not resettle in town.[21]

In calling the population back to the town, Alcalde Sánchez employed a long-standing Spanish urban tradition to secure Laredo's vital interests. Since the sixteenth century Crown decrees had required that all subjects reside in towns and cities, described the conditions for the establishment of urban centers, and even detailed a grid plan by which these should be laid out. Governmental authority in Indian areas also functioned through *cabeceras* and *sujetos* (district seats and dependent towns) in the central region of New Spain and *reducciones* (Indian congregations or villages) for nomadic Indians in the north.[22] As important as the town tradition was in New Spain, the truly compelling reasons for the *alcalde*'s decrees were more immediate. The scattering of Laredo's population weakened the basis for Sánchez's political authority and reduced the value of town properties. It also thinned the line of defense against the Indians, periodically the most pressing problem.

Before the arrival of European settlers on the Rio Grande frontier, the native population survived in the barren region by gathering fruit and seeds and by hunting small game. This marginal existence made their conquest unattractive throughout the seventeenth century. As Spaniards moved north in the eighteenth century, however, they disrupted the Indian way of life by intruding into their territory, subjugating certain groups, and

---

[21] *Bandos* (decrees) issued 6 January 1774, 9 July 1774, 25 August 1775, and 11 January 1781, and Vicente González de Santianes to Tomás Sánchez, 19 August 1775, in Laredo Archives.

[22] Walter D. Harris, *The Growth of Latin American Cities*, pp. 13–14; Mario Góngora, *Studies in the Colonial History of Spanish America*, pp. 98–99, 118–19. Also see Peter Gerhard, *A Guide to the Historical Geography of New Spain*, pp. 36–37.

unintentionally tempting others to partake of Spanish cattle, horses, and crops. In the meantime, the Apaches along the far northern edges of the borderlands had acquired the horse and were in the process of moving south.[23] Thus, pressed from the north and attracted to the south, Comanches and some Apache groups in the upper regions of El Seno Mexicano threatened Laredo's promising future and at times endangered its very existence.

Eventually this menace necessitated the stationing of troops in Laredo. Originally, the settlers had been expected to defend themselves and the northern edges of Nuevo Santander. Don Tomás Sánchez and subsequent *alcaldes* were designated as captains, and the settlers were expected to serve as militiamen. Occasionally they were summoned to give chase to Indians threatening Laredo.[24] But as the Indian meance grew, neither the town nor the province could adequately resist the incursions by the *indios bárbaros*. Royal *visitas* to the borderland regions in the 1760s and 1770s reevaluated defense priorities in the vast area and initiated reforms designed to consolidate Spain's holdings.[25] The resulting peace was expected to stimulate population growth and prosperity, and the establishment of the *presidio*, or garrison, at Laredo resulted in part from this effort.

Officials in neighboring Texas notified the viceroy of alarming reports of losses and deaths at Béxar and Laredo. The governor of Nuevo Santander, Vicente González de Santianes, judged the threat to Laredo to be exaggerated, but as a precaution ordered a contingent of seventeen soldiers and thirty-seven militiamen from other settlements to visit Laredo in 1773 as a show of force. Two years later he assigned a permanent garrison of twenty-two men. The governor expressed the desire that parties

[23] John Francis Bannon, *The Spanish Borderlands Frontier, 1531–1821*, pp. 171–72. The best and most detailed work on Spanish-Indian relationships is Elizabeth A. H. John, *Storms Brewed in Other Men's Worlds: The Confrontation of Indians, Spanish, and French in the Southwest 1540–1795.*

[24] John, *Storms*, p. 438. Oakah L. Jones, Jr., in *Los Paisanos: Spanish Settlers on the Northern Frontier of New Spain*, p. 9, notes that service in the local militia was rendered in lieu of the *alcabala*, or sales tax.

[25] See Max L. Moorhead, *The Apache Frontier*, pp. 16, 33–35; and Moorhead, *The Presidio: Bastion of the Spanish Borderlands*, pp. 61–69, 75–84.

of soldiers and militiamen be sent out periodically to scour the countryside in search of enemy Indians. He assigned a commander for the soldiers, Lieutenant Idelfonso de la Garza, and sent ammunition.[26]

The presence of troops in the town and an occasional campaign to the countryside may have warded off attacks around Laredo. Added vigilance in other towns such as Béxar had diverted the Comanches to the Rio Grande area, but their attacks on the defenseless *ranchos* near Laredo were few. On Ash Wednesday in 1776 two Indian men and a woman actually entered the town and stole a horse. Later that year four Laredoans were killed and one was wounded on the road to Béxar. Two other Laredoans traveling to Béxar were attacked in 1784. On occasion the defenders recaptured some stock and killed an Indian, but for the most part the raiders eluded them. The vast region provided a sanctuary for the Indians, presenting Laredoans with an invisible threat. When the raiders were spotted and a chase ensued, inadequate and exhausted mounts usually prevented Laredoans from apprehending the intruders.[27] As a reprisal for Comanche raids in the area Laredoans launched a forceful assault on an Indian camp in 1780. More than fifty allegedly stolen horses and mules were recovered and two men and a woman were killed. However, the village was inhabited by smallpox-stricken Apaches and not Comanches as first believed.[28]

Other than this single qualified victory, the garrison in Laredo, as elsewhere, operated more to provide a shield against Indian attacks and not as a vanguard of Spanish settlement. The *presidios* in the borderlands, including the one in Laredo, experienced difficulty in recruiting to maintain troop levels and in

[26]Antonio María Bucareli to Barón de Ripperdí, 9 February 1774, in Bexar Archives (cited in John, *Storms*, p. 427); Vicente González Santianes to Tomás Sánchez, 7 December 1773 and 24 December 1775, Laredo Archives.

[27]Vicente González Santianes to Tomás Sánchez, 8 September, 17 September, and 12 October 1776, in Laredo Archives; Athanase de Mézières to Teodoro de Croix, 15 November 1778, and diary of Governor Cabello, 31 January 1784, in Bexar Archives, cited in John, *Storms*, pp. 517, 646.

[28]Governor Cabello to Teodoro de Croix, 20 October 1780, in Bexar Archives, cited in John, *Storms*, p. 629.

equipping, supplying, and paying soldiers. Lack of a strong military tradition, shortage of funds, and the sometimes successful alternative policy of pacifying Indians through gifts postponed the complete overhaul which the reforms had called for.[29]

The limited security afforded by the *presidio* and the small amount of money spent for the garrison by the Crown were not without costs to Laredoans. The townspeople were often expected to pasture the horses from the garrison and at times to quarter the troops. Furthermore, the military, while not primarily responsible for the enforcement of law and order locally, exercised that role nonetheless, and in the 1770s Alcalde Sánchez was obliged to share his authority with the troops' commander. By the same token, the commander shared his authority with Capitán Sánchez. The stage was set for conflict within the town's leadership.[30]

Fear of Lipan Apaches and Comanches seems to have overcome any major controversy, however. Both the *alcalde* and the *capitán* were more concerned with the difficulties of countering the Indian raids than with their overlapping jurisdictions in the town. Their main concern was the lack of cooperation from the neighboring towns and the rural population and the perennial difficulty of pasturing the troops' horses sufficiently close to the garrison to gather them quickly in order to respond to an attack.[31]

Although the *presidio* was formally established, it remains unclear how many soldiers served in it, for how long, and what their relationship was to the Laredo community. There is the possibility that the troops were actually withdrawn and that the commander, who at one time or another may have been a Laredo resident, remained in charge of the local militia. To-

[29] Moorhead, *Presidio*, pp. 112–13, 267–71; Odie B. Faulk, "The Presidio: Fortress or Farce," p. 76.

[30] Vicente González Santianes to Tomás Sánchez, 24 September 1779, in Laredo Archives. Some public facilities were shared on occasion (*Bando* of Miguel Ponce Borrego, 4 July 1789, also in Laredo Archives).

[31] Vicente González Santianes to Tomás Sánchez, 13 June 1775, Cristóbal Baes Benavides to Vicente González Santianes, 21 July 1775, Vicente González Santianes to Tomás Sánchez, 12 April 1776, and decrees of Santiago de Jesús Sánchez, 29 November 1783, and Diego de Lasaga, 21 May 1784, all in Laredo Archives.

wards the end of the century and in the early 1800s town documents refer to Laredo as a *villa* and *presidio* interchangeably. At one point the commander and the mayor were one and the same person (the *capitán alcalde*). The records also mention the presence in Laredo of a *compañía volante*, but it is uncertain whether this was a roving unit made up of soldiers from elsewhere stationed in Laredo or a temporary company of local militiamen or a combination of both.[32]

By the end of the 1780s, the Indian menace, together with the gradual improvement of the Sánchez interests and the acquisition of moderate wealth by a number of Laredo ranchers, reversed the earlier trends toward population dispersion. Despite earlier controversies, some of don Tomás's children married into wealthy families on the west bank, and before the decade had elapsed, Sánchez's chief rival even sided with him in a lawsuit.[33] Sánchez's consolidation and the rise in prominence of a handful of other Laredoans made living in town more attractive. Those who had been seeking economic mobility and security away from the town center slowly but steadily returned to the town to enjoy and display their newly acquired wealth.

The movement of these *rancheros* to the town in turn drew in others who had come to the area. The addition of these newcomers provided Laredo with a healthy, though probably uneven, growth, averaging 6.3 percent annually. The census of 1789, which recorded a population of 708, reflected this migration to the town. Children aged sixteen years and under constituted a relatively small portion of Laredo's population (26.8 percent) in comparison with later years when the proportion of children ranged from 38 percent (1833) to 45 percent (1835). Baptismal and death church records for 1790 point to a very low rate of natural increase (crude) of one per thousand. Single adults made up an extraordinarily large segment (35 percent) of

---

[32] Decree of Joseph Miguel de Cuéllar, 9 March 1803, deed of sale by don Vicente Antonio López Fonseca, 5 December 1805, will of don Cipriano Arizpe, 3 June 1806, and deed of sale by José Ramón Díaz de Bustamante, 11 May 1810, all in Laredo Archives.

[33] Settlement of the estate of don Tomás Sánchez, 5 April 1831, and genealogy of don Tomás Sánchez, in papers of Rev. Florencio Andrés, St. Augustine Catholic Church, Laredo; Joseph Martínez de Sotomayor to Francisco de Vidaurri, 1 July 1777, in Laredo Archives.

inhabitants in 1789, whereas later the proportion of single adults reached a high of only 26.2 percent (1831). These facts suggest a relatively low birthrate and substantial recent immigration.[34]

The physical appearance of the town gave evidence of the growth. The new stone church demonstrated renewed collective prosperity and pride. A few stone and adobe houses, standing in contrast to the large number of one-room *jacales* (stick-and-mud huts with thatched roofs), displayed the existence of a group of distinctly better-off families. These families bartered for or purchased more and a greater variety of foodstuffs than the poor. They also purchased some manufactured tools and even a few items of fine clothing.[35] All of these goods, including most of the food, were brought in from the outside in exchange for wool, hides, and horses. Thus, livestock, which provided the subsistence for the many, was traded by a few for better food and for some tokens of social rank.

As the population of Laredo increased, race and ethnicity apparently became more prominent concerns in the town's society. The census of 1757 had not recorded the ethnicity of the first settlers, but that of 1789 listed Laredo's residents under the categories of *españoles*, Spaniards (45.3 percent), *mestizos*, mixed-bloods (17.2 percent), and *mulatos*, mulattoes (17.2 percent). *Indios*, Indians, enumerated in a completely separate census, composed 15.6 percent of the population. These distinctions were important in Spanish colonial society, and immigrants to the frontier brought them to Laredo.[36]

Presumably the enumerator recorded the reported designation. *Español* was a reference to social rank, and not to peninsular origin, but it may also have been a racial designation. A member of a *visita* party in later years (1828) observed that there were a number of light-complexioned persons among the Laredo

---

[34] Censuses of 1789, 1833, and 1835, in Laredo Archives; baptismal and burial records, St. Augustine Catholic Church, Laredo. For the computation of the crude rate of natural increase, see George W. Barclay, *Techniques of Population Analysis*, pp. 33–37.

[35] Census of 1789; inventory of the estate of Nicolás Campos Castellanos, 27 February 1771, will of José Díaz Tamayo, 24 May 1773, and inventory of the estate of Salvador González Ydalgo, 29 January 1781, in Laredo Archives.

[36] Census of 1789, Laredo Archives. See also, Magnus Mörner, *Race Mixture in the History of Latin America*, pp. 60–62, 97–100.

population. *Indio* implied both race and a separate legal and social status. Despite the sizable *mestizo* population, racial mixture, if any occurred in Laredo, did not take place among legally married partners. Only eighteen persons, or 6.7 percent of all those married, were listed in nine racially mixed marriages. Eight of these involved *españoles* and either *mestizos* or *mulatos*; only one, exclusively members of the *castas* (mixed-blood castes). No marriages between Indians and non-Indians were recorded. Nor were there any marriages between blacks and non-blacks to explain the *mulato* population. It may be that racial mixing had taken place in the interior and not on the frontier.

No record describes the relationship between the various groups, but there is enough evidence to suggest that ethnic and racial distinctions were of consequence in Laredo. Church and government officials listed the designations in most records. A town ordinance in 1770 set fines and punishments according to these distinctions. The very infrequency of racially mixed marriages in general and of marriages between *mulatos* and *mestizos* in particular emphasizes the divisiveness among Laredoans from different castes. Interestingly, enumerators in Laredo continued recording racial and ethnic designations in the unofficial census drafts long after superior authorities no longer required them to do so.[37]

Also of consequence were the titles *don* and *doña*. The exact meaning of these distinctions is not entirely evident, but the censuses of both 1757 and 1789 employ them with some discrimination. In the earlier census two-fifths of the adults were listed with that appellation. In the census of 1789, which records a considerably larger population, only forty-nine *dons* and *doñas* can be distinguished. They and their spouses composed a little over a third of the Spanish adult population. No one other than *españoles* obtained this status and none of the Spanish *dons* married outside their ethnic group.[38]

[37] Decree of 20 May 1770, and drafts of the census of 1835, in Laredo Archives; Luis Berlandier and Rafael Chovel, *Diario de viaje de la comisión de límites que puso el gobierno de la república, bajo la dirección del exmo. sr. general de división d. Manuel de Mier y Terán*, p. 93.

[38] Censuses of 1757 and 1789, in Laredo Archives.

Don and *doña* titles were also used in the baptismal records. Only 35 of the 974 entries made between 1789 and 1809 listed parents who were *dons* and *donās*. Expectedly, the infants baptized in these instances were *españoles*. *Padrinos* (sponsors) who were *dons* and *doñas* participated in twenty-nine of these christenings. Spanish elites also served as sponsors in 48 baptisms of children of Spaniards who were not *dons* and *doñas*. This may indicate some preference for *padrinos* of higher status. There is also the possibility that the sponsors were older persons and that the titles of *don* and *doña* came with seniority rather than merely with wealth. *Dons* and *doñas* served as *padrinos* in only 37 baptisms of individuals who were non-Spaniards.[39]

The separate census for the Indian population symbolized their distinct social and economic role in Laredo. No Indians were mentioned in the census of 1757 or in the report of the Palacio and Ossorio *visita* of 1767. Transient friendly Indians may occasionally have camped near the town, but no settlement of any size was mentioned before 1789, when the census enumerated lll *indios agregados* (settled Indians attached to Spanish town), all Carrizos. They were all baptized and bore Spanish first and last names, and all couples were married in the church. Yet their designation as clustered Indians, their limited participation in religious activity (only a few were admitted into the sacrament of confession), and the total absence of intermarriage between them and other groups suggest that their relationship to the community was socially marginal. Their employment as servants and shepherds and in other low-status occupations and probably their dress and language placed them well below the *mulatos* and *mestizos*. Indians were restricted in their movement, and some may have been held in virtual slavery, as was the girl or woman referred to as an *Indita* in a dispute over property.[40]

[39] Baptismal records, vol. I, St. Augustine Catholic Church, Laredo. *Padrinos* and the child's parents were bound together by the *compadrazgo*, a relationship of coparenting. In practice the *compadrazgo* was used to solidify bonds among friends and acquaintances (See Frances Leon Swadesh, *Los Primeros Pobladores: Hispanic Americans on the Ute Frontier*, pp. 189–92; and Sidney W. Mintz and Eric R. Wolf, "An Analysis of Ritual Parenthood [*Compadrazgo*]," in *Peasant Society, A Reader*, ed. Jack M. Potter et al.).

[40] Note at the bottom of the Indian census of 1789, decree of Miguel Ponce

In the midst of racial, ethnic, and social divisions, the institution of the family stood out as the cohesive factor during the eighteenth century among all groups in Laredo. Although the enumerator in both Indian and non-Indian census reports listed the population according to households, the family structure of Laredo can be reconstructed or at least approximated from the reports.[41] In the non-Indian census a breakdown of all households shows that a vast majority (88.2 percent) were headed by two-parent families. Most of these were single-family households. In only 10 percent of the families did children reside in a one-parent household, and in half of these families that parent was listed as married, although the spouse was not enumerated. In the Indian census all but four of the twenty-five households were headed by couples, and all but two of the households were headed by persons of the same surname, suggesting the possibility that all the Indians belonged to one small band. Thus, *español, mestizo, mulato,* and *indio,* though living in a stratified and divided community, found security and stability in the family unit.[42]

As for the size of the household, it did not vary among the different ethnic groups. In all instances it averaged (mean and median) about four members and remained the same between 1757 and 1789. Of greater consequence was the number of dwellings. There were eighty-five of these by 1789, and they housed an average (mean) of seven persons. Living conditions thus presented problems for individual and family privacy, since

---

Borrego, 5 July 1788, and Tomás Bargas to the Governor, 5 October 1794, in Laredo Archives.

[41] A household in the census is composed of a group of individuals in some way dependent on the head. The group may involve one or two nuclear families (individuals related as husband and wife or parent[s] and children), a family plus single adults, or a single adult heading a unit of other single adults. A second family or boarders, whether related to the head or not, were considered part of the same household unit. Furthermore, members of one household may have lived in more than one dwelling.

[42] Census of 1789, in Laredo Archives. The most ambiguous census category is that of *solteros.* These could be young adults eighteen years of age or older still living with their parents or other related or unrelated boarders. Whatever their relationship to the head of the family, they are so few in this census that the ambiguity of their status does not detract from the conclusion.

jacales were one-room structures, and stone and adobe houses never exceeded three rooms.[43]

Because of housing limitations, social visits between men and women may have often taken place in the *plaza* (town square) or other locations outside the home. Meetings in remote or isolated areas were viewed as socially unacceptable, and the church and civil authorities cooperated to restrict them. Meetings by the river, where women went to wash, were particularly disapproved because the site was away from the town center and also served as the place for bathing. The *justicia mayor* (chief justice), on the curate's advice, attempted to control the situation on several occasions by segregating men and women on the river banks. A curfew that applied to this area and to the town streets also restricted uncondoned trysts. On one occasion an adulterer was banished by the *alcalde*.[44]

Perhaps reflecting these issues was the problem of illegitimacy. One hundred and thirty-six (14 percent) of the 974 infants baptized between 1789 and 1809 were illegitimate. Among *mestizos* the proportion of children born out of wedlock (15.3 percent) was twice that among *españoles* (7 percent), but illegitimacy among *mulatos*, Carrizos, and other Indians was much higher (23.4, 21.4, and 29.8 percent, respectively). Since legitimacy was linked to sacramental matrimony, the high ratio among groups which may have been on the fringe of society is understandable. Nevertheless, the morality of such unions was a serious concern for Laredo's leaders.[45]

The breakdown of law and order was not confined to moral issues related to sexual behavior. A land controversy in 1799 embroiled some Laredoans and resulted in the jailing of one of the parties. The sale of some stolen cloth caused a stir among the

---

[43]Census of 1789, declarations of property for tax purposes of fifteen citizens, 24 August 1815, first will of Petra Sánchez, 23 March 1819, in Laredo Archives.

[44]City ordinances, Santiago de Jesús Sánchez, 2 May 1782, Miguel Ponce Borrego, 5 July 1788 and 6 September 1788, decree of José Antonio Farías, 29 April 1809, all in Laredo Archives.

[45]*Mestizo* illegitimate children composed 42.6 percent of all infants born out of wedlock. For the link betwen illegitimacy and the *mestizage* (racial mixture) process, see Mörner, *Race Mixture*, pp. 40–45.

townspeople in the summer of 1805. A ghastly murder following a dance in the summer of 1809 disturbed the town's peaceful existence, and the robbery of 400 pesos from the priest's house in 1812 shocked everyone. Periodically the authorities resorted to declaring curfews, forbidding the carrying of firearms, and requiring the registration of strangers.[46]

Laredo's law and order difficulties were symptomatic of regional problems. From 1797 to 1809 the *alcalde* received warrants for the arrest of criminals wanted for offenses committed elsewhere in Nuevo Santander and in the nearby provinces. Presumably growth and population movements prevented the rigid control exercised in communities in the area before this period.[47]

As a response to the new problems and as an expression of new political and social loyalties, church and state entered a period of harmony in Laredo. Harmony in the relationship between the church and civil authorities was more than an expression of mutual ideals for an orderly society. It was a sharing of political and social loyalties. This had not been so during the life of the first curate, a Revillano who sided with the faction from the west bank. But his successor, don José María García, came from the families allied with Sánchez interests, and conflicts with the *alcalde* and *cabildo* disappeared. In fact, the *alcalde* threatened Laredoans with eight days in jail if they did not assist in building the priest's house. Whereas in other communities the missionary or the priest appointed by the bishop represented an external power and sometimes competed with local leaders in making decisions that affected the social structure of the town, in Laredo the *cura* (parish priest) and *alcalde* worked

---

[46] María Alejandra Sánchez to the governor, 25 February 1799, report of the investigation of the stolen cloth, 11 June 1805, report to the governor of José Lafuente, 20 August 1809, report to the governor of Miguel Sánchez Navarro Palos, 9 January 1812, and decrees of 29 May 1779, 15 November 1783, 6 September 1788, 22 August 1790, in Laredo Archives.

[47] José González de Siendas to the *alcaldes*, 4 February 1797, fragments of descriptions of fugitives, 27 February 1803, warrants for the arrest of various criminals, warrants for the arrest of Pedro Cabrera, 4 March, Euselio Aguirre, 29 April, José Francisco Rodríquez and Manuel Galindo, 3 and 17 July, and Pedro Bulnes, 1 November 1809, all in Laredo Archives.

hand in hand to preserve an order threatened only by outside forces, whether Indians, soldiers, or newcomers.[48]

At times authority came into conflict with local concerns. In practice the *alcalde* received and posted regularly all the decrees of the king and the viceroy that circulated on the frontiers, but those which interfered with well-established traditions he did not enforce. For example, Crown regulations forbidding card games and the sale of mescal and tobacco were ignored because they proposed changing favored pastimes and disrupted important economic activities. On one occasion in 1816 the town's authorities were more preoccupied with settling a quarrel over credit and family honor than illegal gambling. In fact, the only recorded instance of any action taken to uphold Crown regulations occurred when a crafty mescal vendor from out of town dealt the local card players out of their hard-earned pesos. Restrictions on the sale of tobacco were also evaded. Merchants offered cigars and cigarettes free as *pilón*, a promotional incentive to circumvent the royal monopoly. Thus, the Crown's designs for a well-ordered community met with serious obstacles unless they coincided with the interest of the townspeople.[49]

Survival, not maintenance of law and order, was Laredo's main problem. While cattle grazing and horse trading brought prosperity to some, limited local food production and the shortage of currency presented formidable difficulties for almost everyone. Small strips of river bottomland provided a modicum of economic independence to a few landowners, but most of the population depended upon food supplied by a handful of *carreteros*. These teamsters also brought from interior Mexico cloth and metal goods, which they traded in Laredo by means of barter and credit.[50]

---

[48] *Bando* of 6 January 1774, in Laredo Archives. Church-state controversies, such as those in New Mexico and Texas, revolved around the control over sources of wealth (land and Indians) (Bannon, *Spanish Borderlands Frontier*, pp. 80–81, 234–235).

[49] Decree of 15 November 1783, suit of Gabriel Tovar against Don Rafael Oropresa, 6 May 1816, and Santiago de Jesús Sánchez to Captain José de la Garza, 6 May 1899, all in Laredo Archives.

[50] José González to Manuel Ygnacio de Escandón, 7 July 1797, and testimony of Leonardo Sánchez, 19 July 1783, in Laredo Archives.

Availability of credit was a special problem for Laredoans and for all who lived on the frontier. Because of the lack of specie, well-to-do families often owed each other money. Hardly a will exists that does not mention debts and credits, with amounts often listed in terms of stock or goods. While credit made food and the amenities of life available to many Laredoans, it produced a considerable amount of friction in the isolated community. Quarrels over money sometimes led to the jailing of neighbors and to strained relationships between the military and civilians.[51]

The problems related to credit undoubtedly resulted from Laredo's economic difficulties. In 1795 Félix Calleja reported that Laredo's population had risen to 636, reflecting an average annual rate of growth of less than 1 percent since the census of 1789. The town's economic resources had risen, but not proportionately to the population. Only wealth in cattle remained on the same per-capita level reported in 1757, the last census rendering such information. Per-capita sheep and goats plummeted from 106.8 to 14.5.[52]

Economic difficulties may have also been the stimulus for the population shifts in the late eighteenth and early nineteenth centuries. Parish baptismal records suggest that Spaniards, *mulatos*, and Carrizo Indians either experienced lower birthrates than other groups or began leaving Laredo in the period after 1789. From that date, when the registry begins, to 1809 the priest christened 972 infants and two adults. The proportion of Spaniards, *mulatos*, and Carrizos among those baptized during this period is considerably lower than their respective representation among both the entire population and the heads of households enumerated in 1789. Whatever the cause for this variation, Laredo's population appears to have been in flux. The outbreak of the War of Independence would only aggravate this.[53]

[51] Vincente Antonio Para to Lt. Governor Antonio Cordero, 2 May 1789, Rafael López de Oropeza to Jesús María Tovar, 2 April 1817, Petra Sánchez Uribe to José Fernando Vidaurri, 20 April 1795, Magdalena Gutiérrez to Manuel de Escandón, 24 January 1795, and Enríque Camilo Juárez to the captain of the Tercera Compañía Volante, 20 September 1805, all in Laredo Archives.

[52] Vigness, "Nuevo Santander in 1795," p. 464.

[53] Baptismal and burial records, St. Augustine Catholic Church, Laredo.

CHAPTER 2

War and Social Change, Prosperity and Recession, 1810–35

THE sound of the bell Father Miguel Hidalgo rang on the morning of September 16, 1810, signaling the opening of the Mexican War of Independence, was heard in the remote corners of New Spain's borderland frontier. There, the same tinder existed that inspired the uprising nationally—divisions among ethnic and racial groups, excesses or neglect by the central authority, and frustrations of upwardly mobile *criollos* ("Spaniards" born in the New World); and the tinder was ready to be ignited. By 1811, revolt had spread to Nuevo Santander and the surrounding provinces. From the Rio Grande settlements, José Bernardo Gutiérrez de Lara, a Revillano descendant of an old Coahuila family, stirred the fires with proclamations and propaganda that encouraged the downfall of the Loyalist governor at Aguayo, the capital of Nuevo Santander. To the east, Juan Bautista de las Casas led a garrison coup in Béxar that captured the governor and Texas for the Insurgents. In Coahuila, too, rebels took the provincial government easily.[1] The northeast frontier seemed ablaze with revolutionary fervor and appeared securely in the Hidalgo camp.

But most of these revolts turned out to be weak and premature. In a short time the counterrevolutionaries won back the northern provinces and engineered the capture of Hidalgo himself. Nevertheless, the sentiment for independence was kept alive. Gutiérrez de Lara and some Texas patriots traveled the back roads to Louisiana in search of men, money, and moral sup-

[1] José Bernardo Gutiérrez de Lara, "Gutiérrez de Lara to the Mexican Congress," in *The Papers of Mirabeau Buonaparte Lamar*, ed. Charles Adams Gulick, Jr., and others, I, 5; Félix D. Almaráz, *Tragic Cavalier*, pp. 118–19; Julia Kathryn Garrett, *Green Flag Over Texas*, pp. 34–35.

port for a second attempt to wrench the northern provinces from Spanish control. With the aid of American filibusters under William Augustus Magee, Gutiérrez de Lara recaptured Béxar in 1813, kindling the hopes of providing a corridor leading to other rebels in the interior. But the victory was only temporary, and Spanish officials held on tenaciously to the borderlands until events in the central region of New Spain changed the course of history for them.[2]

When pressed to take a stand, Laredo's *cabildo* pledged its allegiance to the Crown in August, 1811. Because the *presidio* had remained loyal, the *regidores* (aldermen) had no alternative but to follow suit. The resolution was a formality only; there was no effective participation by Laredoans in the struggle. The members of the propertied class, confident of their position within the town, relied on the garrison to protect their interests from Indian raids. To have sided with the Insurgents, the town leaders would have risked being dislodged by the troops or, perhaps worse, left defenseless at the mercy of the *indios bárbaros*. Yet, regardless of what banner Laredoans rallied under, or which side won the war, the town lost just the same. The conflagration on the frontier eventually required troop redeployments that left the town without adequate protection. War also brought in new people who changed the makeup of the frontier communities. The result for Laredo was a decade of economic depression and social disruption.[3]

The war ended when Insurgents and Loyalists put aside political differences and settled on the common goal of independence, but the fragile compromises soon came apart. Iturbide's claim to the crown of a new empire sparked the development of

---

[2] Garrett, *Green Flag Over Texas*, pp. 67–70; "Gutiérrez de Lara to the Mexican Congress," in Gulick and others, *Papers of Lamar*, I, 5; Almaráz, *Tragic Cavalier*, pp. 170–73; Félix D. Almaráz, "Governor Antonio Martínez and Mexican Independence in Texas: An Orderly Transition," *Permian Historical Annual* 15 (December, 1975): 48–50.

[3] José Antonio Benavides to don Félix María Calleja del Rey, 1 August 1811. There were calls to arms (decrees of Joseph Ramón Díaz de Bustamante, 11 November 1810, and José González, 9 March 1813), but there was little action taken (José Antonio de Cuéllar to José María Tovar, 29 June 1815, in Laredo Archives, St. Mary's University of San Antonio).

political parties along the lines of preindependence positions: Centralists, formerly the Loyalists, whose economic and political power was centered in Mexico City, favored a national government similar to that of New Spain, while Federalists, previously the Insurgents, represented the interests of the fringe areas and preferred decentralization and states' rights. Preoccupation with this conflict, at the core of the rise and fall of Iturbide, resulted in neglect of the frontier by the national government.[4] Though uninvolved in the immediate political struggle, Laredo nonetheless suffered the consequences. Only when the political attacks were quieted somewhat with the acceptance of the Constitution of 1824 did the frontier receive attention. For a few years after that Laredo enjoyed the fruits of peace, prospering and growing at rates similar to those in the early years of the town's settlement.

By the 1830s, however, Laredo's prosperity was again threatened by Indian attacks. Apaches and Comanches, now better armed because of the American commercial presence in the Mexican borderlands, renewed their campaigns along the Rio Grande under pressures from the growing Indian population on the plains. Several tribes originally located east of the Mississippi had been pushed to the west before 1810.[5] After the war, Mexican Federalists supported the immigration of American settlers into Texas, thereby furthering the American westward movement, which indirectly intensified Indian problems. The situation became more critical when the Texans revolted against Mexico and war returned to the area. The new conflict upset the economy of the frontier and weakened defenses against the Indians. Laredo's post-1824 prosperity then turned into depression.[6]

[4] Charles A. Hale, *Liberalism in the Age of Mora, 1821–1853*, pp. 19–22; William Spence Robertson, *Iturbide of Mexico*, pp. 193–94; Leopoldo Zea, "La ideología liberal y el liberalismo en México," in *El liberalismo y la reforma en México*, pp. 489–91. Also see Justo Sierra, *Evolución política del pueblo mexicano*, pp. 196–98; and Vito Alessio Robles, *Coahuila y Texas desde la consumación de la independencia hasta el tratado de Guadalupe Hidalgo*, I, 157–58, 166–70.

[5] W. W. Newcomb, *The Indians of Texas*, pp. 340–41.

[6] Eugene C. Barker, *Mexico and Texas, 1821–1835*, pp. 18–19; Zea, "La ideología liberal y el liberalismo en México," pp. 489–91; Alessio Robles, *Coahuila y Texas*, II, 239–43.

War and Social Change

The crises in 1808–10 in Spain and in the New World, like other major events, seemed at first not to affect Laredo. The *alcalde* was informed of the creation of the Spanish Cortes (parliament) and the election of representatives from the province, but the notice arrived too late for Laredo and the other river towns to vote. The town leaders made no comment on the imposition of Napoleon's brother Joseph on the Spanish throne or on the report of Hidalgo's revolt. Decrees aimed at stemming the insurrection encouraged Laredoans and residents of the river towns to travel to Béxar to assist in defending that outpost. Priests were told to preach loyalty to the Indians, and officials were instructed to have the Indians make bows and arrows in the event that they would have to assist in the protection of the borderlands. Again there was no recorded official reaction; nor is there any indication that any of these precautions were taken in Laredo.[7]

At the outbreak of Hidalgo's revolt Laredo's allegiance to the Crown may have been taken for granted since for almost a year no statement of support was issued, but the widening of the conflict created the need for tighter security, assurances of loyalty, and pledges of assistance. In June, 1811, Commandant General Joaquín de Arredondo decreed new regulations for the towns which forbade the carrying of arms, the sale of intoxicating beverages, and public dances. He also restricted movement within the province. Later that summer Laredoans sent the commandant the first confirmation of their loyalty and reported the formation of six companies. But there is no evidence to indicate whether Arredondo's restrictions were enforced or whether the militia units were deployed at that time or existed only on paper.[8]

By fall the town began to experience the effects of the war.

[7] Manuel de Iturbe y Yraeta to the *alcalde*, 20 September 1810, decrees of 27 September and 12 October 1810, and Joseph Ramón Díaz de Bustamante to the *alcalde*, 16 and 21 November 1810, all in Laredo Archives. For a discussion of the *cortes* in the New World, see Nettie Lee Benson, *Mexico and the Spanish Cortes, 1810–1822.*

[8] Decree of Joaquín de Arredondo, 22 August 1811, and José Antonio Benavides to Joaquín de Arredondo, 25 August 1811, in Laredo Archives.

Laredoans found themselves without soap, sugar, cloth, food items, and according to José Manuel Pérez, worst of all, without tobacco. The prospect of acquiring these and other items did not appear good since the trade fair at Saltillo had been cancelled. The following spring Laredoans were pressured to increase their contribution to the war effort, but the *alcalde* defended the town's role by explaining that Laredoans were serving at the garrison, taking sentry duty, going on patrols, and guarding the mail to Béxar and other points. The need to issue a second call to arms in 1813 belies the *alcalde's* earlier report, however. All males fifteen to sixty years of age were ordered to assemble in the town square with whatever weapons they had in order to be organized into companies. But again there is no report that any action was taken. Apparently some assistance was given against insurgent neighbor José Bernardo Gutiérrez de Lara in 1813, but no records exist describing the extent of Laredo's participation.[9]

The spread of revolt to the frontier may have inspired plans to reinforce the garrison of Laredo. An extant map depicts a moat and wall around Laredo, nine barracks and fortifications along the wall, and a tower guarding the ferry and ford of the river. The document, a copy of a plan designed in 1813 by an officer of the second Flying Company of Nuevo Santander, is misleading because it implies that all the structures actually existed, although there is no record of any of them. While some barracks may have existed, there is no reference to a moat, wall, or tower in any prior or subsequent document in the Laredo Archives or elsewhere. In all likelihood the map detailed a suggested fortification of Laredo.[10]

The crisis deepened at the end of the decade when the turmoil of the War of Independence and Indian raids engulfed the countryside around Laredo. In July, 1819, the presidial captain requested assistance from the *alcalde* to launch an offensive against the Indians, but the campaign was ineffective or may not

---

[9] José Manuel Pérez to José Ramón Díaz de Bustamante, 10 September 1811, José Lázaro Benavides to José Ramón Díaz de Bustamante, 28 April 1812, and decree of Joseph González, 9 March 1813, all in Laredo Archives.

[10] Map of the *presidio* de Laredo, 1813, in Archives of the State of Nuevo León (copy provided by Adán Benavides).

have gotten off the ground at all because the attacks on the town continued. Laredoans began to leave in such numbers that by late summer the *alcalde* had used up the blank passports previously sent by the governor and was in need of more. The exodus further strained the town's defenses, and by fall travel became extremely dangerous. One soldier and two residents were killed in September, and all were cautioned to stay within the town. Within a year Laredo was in shambles from the constant warfare.[11]

Aggravating the depression was a high dependency ratio. The census of 1819 listed a total of 786 dependent individuals (657 children aged sixteen and under and 129 adults aged fifty-one or older) and 632 in the productive age group, of which 289 were males. The dependency ratio was 124; that is, there were 124 dependents for each 100 productive members. The previous census in 1789 did not provide the age distributions necessary to make an exact comparison. However, a comparison of children sixteen years of age or under to all adults (seventeen or older) can be made. In such groups children in 1819 constituted 45.6 percent of the Spanish population and 46.8 percent of the non-Spanish population as against 24.9 and 28.4 respectively in 1789.

Reacting to the crisis, *rancheros* abandoned the *corridas* (roundups) and brought their herds close to town. Some left the Laredo area altogether; others turned to farming the river bottomlands. But good land was scarce, and the danger of Indian attack kept many from venturing far from the settlement. Those tilling the more remote plots attended their *milpas* (cornfields) only at planting and harvesting time. In spite of growing more maize, Laredoans continued to depend on muleteers to import large amounts of grain and other staples. But money to pay for these goods was scarce because the *vaqueros* were employed cultivating the land rather than obtaining valuable hides in the

[11]José María Echeagaray to Idelfonso Ramón, 17 May 1819, and Ramón to Echeagaray, 18 September 1819, Juan José Llamas to Ramón, 21 and 28 July 1819, Echeagaray to *alcalde*, 8 October 1819, and José Antonio Benavides to the governor (?), 16 July 1820, all in Laredo Archives. Indians were accused of collaborating and supporting the insurgents (Decree of Joaquín de Arredondo, 11 April 1815, and Francisco Galván to *alcalde*, 14 March and 8 July 1815, also in Laredo Archives).

hinterlands where Indians roamed. Faced with the reduced buying power of the townspeople, merchants cut back on their inventories, and artisans, faring even worse, closed their shops and took up plowing. Some Laredoans defied royal decrees and transported cartloads of contraband tobacco to the interior. All Laredoans faced a variety of changes in their lives and in their community.[12]

Quarrels among Laredoans over debts and inheritances, conflicts with neighboring towns, and discord among the officials became more frequent as the war progressed. In the previous period credit, as suggested by the appearance of debts in wills and inventories, was used to circumvent the lack of currency; in the war years debts became issues in public disturbances and litigations. Latent rivalries among the river towns surfaced as communities were vexed by increasing responsibilities. Officials, too, were under more intense pressure, and the harmony between the *alcalde* and the presidial and provincial authorities was disrupted. The captain complained that the townspeople were not helping to guard cargoes going to Béxar and that they were not turning over wild livestock to the military. The governor rebuked Laredoans for their lack of cooperation. Also, possibly reacting to the lack of compliance on the part of Laredoans to a *prestamo forzozo* (forced loan) levied to meet the province's war obligations, the governor ordered Laredoans to repay the debts owed the estate of Gutiérrez de Lara.[13]

Laredo's economic woes may have given rise to a wave of

[12]Censuses of 1789 and 1819, *expediente* (file) of Silvestre Díaz de la Vega, 3 May 1800, and José Andrés Farías to Juan José Llamas, 24 August 1818, in Laredo Archives. Because not everyone in the productive age groups is economically active and because some members of the dependent age group are, a dependency ratio is only an estimate, but it has been proven to be a good one (See George W. Barclay, *Techniques of Population Analysis*, pp. 267, 272).

[13]On the matter of controversies over debt see declaration of María Brígida Sánchez, 7 September 1812, José Ynocente Treviño to Señor Subdelegado de la Villa de Laredo, 23 December 1818, José Antonio Benavides to Victoriano Dovalina, 10 March 1820, and case of Leandro San Miguel versus José María González and Gertrudis Villarreal, 10 June 1822, all in Laredo Archives. Also unprecedented was the involvement of two prominent families in a suit over a breach of contract (charges against Idelfonso Ramón lodged by Gertrudis Villarreal, 20 November 1820) and the inheritance quarrels, including one over the estate of don Tomás Sánchez (declarations of Santos Peres de Gaytán,

banditry in the countryside. New regulations had to be issued to protect what was left of the cattle and sheep grazing industry and the mustang roundup. To prevent theft and insure the payment of taxes, unsupervised slaughtering of cattle was prohibited, but the law was sometimes ignored. Neighbors from Palafox, above Laredo, and from Revilla complained that Laredoans were rustling cattle. The open range and the large numbers of cattle complicated the situation. Many owners could not even estimate the extent of their livestock holdings. The *rodeo* technique of gathering livestock also furnished opportunities for theft. To prevent this, the roundup itself had to be authorized and all stock brought to the Laredo plaza. There, the branded animals were returned to their owners. Of those unclaimed, some were turned over to the Crown for taxes and the others were divided among the *vaqueros*.[14]

A virtual population shuffle took place within Laredo during the turbulent war years. The census of 1819 records 1,418 people in Laredo, more than double the 708 of 1789. But the rate of increase over the thirty years had averaged only 2.3 percent annually, much less than before 1789. Since this reduction occurred at a time when the birthrate appears to have been higher than before and immigration continued, it is clear that many Laredoans emigrated. Those who left, Spaniards, *mestizos*, *mulatos*, and Indians—all more or less in the same proportion—were mostly young persons aged seventeen to twenty-five years, who left to seek opportunities elsewhere. Immigrants to Laredo belonged to the same ethnic and racial backgrounds as those who left, but were older, aged twenty-six to forty. They barely replaced those leaving, and the once-energetic growth of the town slowed down considerably.[15]

---

2 September 1817, and Dolores de Rivera, 26 October 1818, Teodosio González to José Antonio Benavides, 13 March 1820, and Manuel Francisco Pérez versus heirs of Tomás Sánchez, 6 June 1822, all also in Laredo Archives).

[14] *Bando*, 27 December 1815, Enrique García to Idelfonso Ramón, 24 April 1819, José Bernardino Benavides to Idelfonso Ramón, 17 May 1819, Leonardo Sánchez to *alcalde*, 19 July 1783, *bando* of Melchor Vidal de Lorca y Villena, 21 June 1780, and José María de Echeagaray to Idelfonso Ramón, 25 August 1819, all in Laredo Archives.

[15] The exact birthrate for the period betwen 1789 and 1819 cannot be determined, but the large base cohort, from infancy to age seven, suggests a high rate. By the same

There was no appreciable change in Laredo's population between 1819 and 1820, but shifts in the population structure continued and the racial character of the town changed significantly. Perhaps because of the defeat of the insurgents in the north, Spaniards from other areas moved to Laredo, netting an annual increase of 30.6 percent for that group and making *españoles* the majority in the community. Spaniards comprised 45.3 percent of the town's population in 1789, 43.3 percent in 1819, and 57.2 percent in 1820. Most of the new Spanish settlers were adults aged seventeen to forty-nine years, with very small, young families. Indians, *mestizos*, and *mulatos*, largely young adults with families larger than those of Spaniards, may have moved back to the *rancherías* (settlement clusters) and to other towns. They left Laredo in such numbers that the non-Spanish population fell by 23.9 percent.[16]

The smaller the numbers of Indians and mixed-bloods, the fewer restraints they could place on attempts by upper-class *españoles* to cut their losses in times of depression by exacting more from workers, especially indebted servants. Indebtedness resulting from the economic difficulties quite naturally brought the greatest hardships to the Indians and the poor. While it is difficult to estimate the extent of peonage, crisis in the system developed after the turn of the century, in the period of the conflict for independence. Complaints sprang up at that time involving adult peons and children who had been entrusted as security for debts. Peons usually complained of maltreatment and virtual enslavement through continual debt.[17] As might be ex-

---

token, the unexpectedly large cohorts aged twenty-six to forty indicate a sizable immigration. The source of migration into Laredo is unknown, although earlier there had been reports of people from Palafox moving into Laredo (censuses of 1789 and 1819, Ygnacio Elizondo to José Manuel García and José María Benavides to Elizondo, 2 April 1813, all in Laredo Archives. See Donald J. Bogue, *Principles of Demography*, pp. 149–53).

[16] Censuses of 1789, 1819, 1820, and 1823, in Laredo Archives. The census of 1823 no longer provided a racial breakdown. The size and age of the families is an approximation arrived at by comparing the births as recorded in the baptismal records (St. Augustine Catholic Church, Laredo) and the numbers added or missing in the sex-age categories.

[17] María Brígida Sánchez to Lorenzo Sánchez de la Cortina, 17 August 1811, Santiago Peña to Idelfonso Ramón, 15 February 1819, and Juan Echandía to Idelfonso Ramón, 11 November 1815, all in Laredo Archives.

pected, lenders lamented the fact that indebted servants did not work diligently, were disobedient, and ran away easily. Surprisingly, the authorities often were sympathetic to the woes of the debtors and did not invariably side with the lender.[18] The conflicts over credit, nevertheless, sounded a note of discord within the community that echoed the conflict over independence along the frontier.

Also affected by the constant flow of people through Laredo were sexual relationships, courtship patterns, and family life. In 1789 men outnumbered women in Laredo, a common feature of growing frontier communities. By 1819 the situation had reversed. The earlier ratio among adults of 105 males for every 100 females plummeted to 84 to 100. The exodus of men left behind an increasing number of fatherless families. In 1789, more than nine-tenths of all heads of families were in husband-and-wife and two-parent families; by 1819, the proportion of married household heads may have dropped to about three-fourths.[19] The absence of men also caused problems for single women of marriageable age. In the four-year span between 1819 and 1823, the available young single men of marriageable age declined almost 10 percent annually.[20] An imbalance in the sex ratios had not been a problem for Laredo before the war; the new ratios recorded in the wartime censuses reflect the extent of the social disruption caused by the conflict.

[18] Suit of José Santiago Pérez against don Manuel Pérez ("Su amo," his master), 5 February to 2 March 1819, Idelfonso Ramón to Bernardo Benavides, 4 April 1819, and José Antonio Benítez to José Francisco de la Garza, 16 and 19 October and 13 November 1818 (wherein is discussed the problem of a runaway Indian woman and the need for cooperation between the different towns), all in Laredo Archives. In two cases the use of physical force by the lender cancelled the debt owed by the peon (Ramón Pérez to José María Tovar, 1 August 1815, and agreement between don Manuel Pérez, Santiago Peña, and Idelfonso Ramón, 15 August 1819). In still another case the governor ruled that in the event of serious personal conflict the peonage debt could be paid with money earned by working for another party (Joaquín de Arredondo to José María Tovar, 5 January 1815, Laredo Archives).

[19] This is an approximation because the census of 1819 does not provide the family and household information given in the census of 1789. However, those listed as married in 1819 compose 77.4 percent of all persons in both married and widowed categories.

[20] Marriage age must have been at or above seventeen. Only two persons married under this age, one male and one female, are listed in the census reports during this period and the next.

In contrast to earlier censuses, which had not listed any widows, wartime tallies record a large number of women in that category.[21] Unfortunately, the available documents do not disclose whether the widows had been the spouses of deceased soldiers, or *rancheros*, or Laredoans, or a combination of these.[22] The lack of official comment concerning widows, together with the absence of any report indicating a disproportionate death rate among males, presents the alternate possibility that many of the census "widows" were actually abandoned married women, unwed mothers, or women living in common-law marriages. Given the norms set by the community, these women may have designated themselves as "widows" to avoid embarrassment, or the census enumerator may have used the term as a euphemism. If this was the case, or even if they were in fact widows, the consequences of the war on Laredo's society were as serious as the combat fatalities themselves.

The dramatic increase in illegitimacy as described in the baptismal records reflects this problem. Between 1810 and 1817 the percentage of illegitimate children ranged from 9.1 to 16.5; between 1818 and 1823 it ranged from 29.5 to 45.1, considerably higher than the peak of 26.9 percent in prewar years (1789). High incidence of illegitimacy occurred among all ethnic groups, including Spaniards, who in the previous period had relatively fewer illegitimate children than *mestizos, mulatos*, Indians, and *castas*.[23]

Common-law unions were denounced by the *alcalde* in 1816 as a menace to the community's well-being. On one occasion an emotional controversy arose when the priest asked the mayor to exert pressure for parental approval on marriage in-

---

[21] It is conceivable that the Laredo census listed so many widows because of their migration from the countryside to the town where they could receive assistance from relatives or expect to earn their livelihood. Christen I. Archer, *The Army in Bourbon Mexico, 1760–1810*, p. 225, attributes the presence of large numbers of widows in earlier censuses in the central region of New Spain to attempts by men and their families to avoid military service. This is certainly not the case in Laredo.

[22] Among single adults ages seventeen to forty years, males (110) outnumber females (84), but when single and widowed adults in that age group are considered together (males, 112; females, 120), this disparity in the sex ratio is reversed (Census of 1819, in Laredo Archives).

[23] Baptismal and burial records, St. Augustine Catholic Church, Laredo.

volving minors coming from different social backgrounds who were already living together. Also during this period two unprecedented cases came up involving charges against individuals who had disrupted marriage relationships. The turnover in the population stimulated by ups and downs of the war altered the texture of the social structure and exacerbated moral problems in the community.[24]

The end of the war in 1821 did not bring immediate economic recovery and peace to Laredo. The town and the frontier, though far removed from Mexico City, suffered the consequences of the political strife that kept the central government from providing adequate defense against Indians and forceful direction to the economy. The halt in the town's growth between 1819 and 1820 turned into a loss by 1823, when the population fell to 1,402, from 1,430 in 1820. The decline was very small, less than 1 percent annually, but it was indicative of worsening conditions. The population shifts persisted, though they were not as dramatic as before. Among those aged eight through forty years the proportion of males to females dropped gradually but constantly in the four-year period. From this and other shifts in the sex and age cohorts and from the marital statistics, it appears that the permanent population was small. High birthrates for 1819 and 1823 (42.3 and 49.2 per thousand) offset the lack of growth through immigration.[25]

In spite of all the difficulties besetting the town, a school was opened in 1822 for the male children of Laredo. Earlier efforts to establish a school had failed. The schoolmaster, Francisco Fernández, in his reports to the *cabildo*, recorded the progress of his students through different stages of reading and writing. He did not teach arithmetic, or at least did not report

[24] Decree of José Andrés Farías, 14 July 1816, José de Jesús Sánchez to Idelfonso Ramón, 21 August 1819, José María García to Idelfonso Ramón, 6 and 13 September 1819, decree of José Francisco de la Garza, 12 January 1824, case against Gregorio García, 28 February to 24 March 1824, all in Laredo Archives.

[25] So as not to allow the fluctuations in the number of births to distort the rates (since fluctuations would loom large in a small population such as Laredo's), the number of births in the years 1818 to 1821 were averaged to calculate the rate for 1819–20, and the years 1822 and 1824 were averaged to calculate the rate for 1823 (Baptismal records, St. Augustine Catholic Church, Laredo).

the levels of achievement in arithmetic to the city fathers, but he did teach logic and civics by reading and explaining a chapter a day from the Spanish Constitution of 1812. A handful of his students were withdrawn by their parents because they objected to the schoolmaster's methods of discipline.[26] But the September enrollment of sixty-six students remained fairly constant until March, when it was cut in half because the garrison's payroll was suspended and the children of the military families could no longer attend.[27] Enrollment continued low during the 1823–24 term, but rose again the following year when Laredo prospered and population grew in the peaceful postwar period. The new students must have included many who could not pay the tuition, however, because the town requested state funds to educate the poor.[28]

Governmental transition from colony to empire and later to republic created some difficulties on the frontier, but on the whole the transfer of power was smooth in Laredo. Authorities received notice of the success of the independence movement, the threat of reconquest, the establishment of the empire, Iturbide's downfall, and the call for the constitutional convention, but no official comment was made. Difficulties with the mail system made Laredo's endorsement of the creation of the republic come among the last. The issue that did attract their attention was the possibility that Laredo and other river towns would be incorporated into the state of Nuevo León. Laredoans favored this, perhaps because of Nuevo Santander's neglect of the settlers and town-dwellers in that northeastern corner of the province. The integrity of the new state of Tamaulipas was preserved, how-

---

[26] According to the schoolmaster, the parents were unwilling to allow him to discipline the children effectively (Francisco Fernández to the *cabildo*, 1 October 1822, in Laredo Archives).

[27] Francisco Fernández to the *cabildo*, 1 April 1823, and José Lázaro Benavides, decree of 13 May 1827, in Laredo Archives.

[28] Monthly reports of the schoolmaster to the *cabildo*, October–December, 1822, January–July, 1823, October–December, 1824, April–December, 1828, and January, May–December, 1829, in Laredo Archives. Whether the gaps in the reports represent interruptions in the functioning of the school is uncertain. For the request for state assistance see José María Tovar to José Francisco de la Garza, 13 February 1824, also in the Laredo Archives.

ever, and the question seemed moot by the time Laredoans celebrated the birth of the new republic.[29]

On the morning of January 31, 1824, townspeople and soldiers gathered in the plaza to witness the *cabildo* take the oath
of loyalty. After the ceremony, peals of bells and gun salutes
filled the air while the assembly proceeded to the church to sing
the Te Deum and assist at mass. A parade and other demonstra-
tions of jubilation followed. The official celebration lasted the
customary three days. The formation of the republic no doubt
inspired hope of a lasting peace that would usher in prosperity
and reestablish Laredo's stability.[30]

Within the very year of the new constitution the town's
population increased from 1,402 to 1,570, a growth rate of 12 percent. A large migration of single individuals aged twenty-six to
thirty-nine years and more moderate increases among married
persons in that same age group and among children aged seven
to sixteen years account for most of the growth. While these increases may have forecast better times, the slight declines in all
other sex-age groups in the three marital categories serve as a
reminder that the disturbances created by the war were still affecting Laredo.[31]

Prosperity and Recession

By 1828, four years after the creation of the republic, Laredo's
growth began to resemble that of the early years of expansion.
The census of 1828 recorded 2,052 persons, reflecting a 7 percent average annual increase for the period since 1824, the highest rate in thirty years. The most impressive growth occurred
among the married persons aged seventeen to twenty-five years,
a group which zoomed from 2 persons to 159. The number of

[29] Decrees of the governor, 11 August and 12 September 1822, José Ignacio de la
Peña, 12 April 1823, José María Tovar to the governor, 26 December 1823, Ayunta-
miento, señor Cura y otras personas to the governor, 31 March 1823, José Ignacio Fernández to the *alcalde*, 17 June 1823, and decree of Juan Francisco Gutiérrez, 14 February
1824, all in Laredo Archives.

[30] Report of José Francisco de la Garza to the governor, 14 March 1824, in Laredo
Archives.

[31] Census of 1824, in Laredo Archives.

children under six years rose by 13 percent annually, and the number of young single men aged seventeen to twenty-five years increased by 18.4 percent. All married sex-age groups increased at almost twice the rate of the entire population. The birthrate rose from 48.5 per thousand in 1824 and 31.8 in 1825 to 60.7 in 1826, 68.6 in 1827, and 63.2 in 1828.[32] The presence of married individuals in such large numbers in the 1828 census coupled with a rise in the birthrate suggests a marked increase in early marriages or an extensive migration into Laredo of young families. Either response confirms the supposition of secure, steady progress in Laredo since 1824.

Accompanying this growth and perhaps stimulating it was a sharp increase in sheep grazing. In the mid-1820s Laredoans turned in greater number to tending flocks, which increased from 700 head in 1824 to 3,223 four years later (an average annual rate of 46.5 percent). Wool replaced hides as the major source of wealth and became Laredo's chief export commodity. An average annual increase of only 14.3 percent in the number of mules suggests that wool was more important than hides.

The production of wool created a greater dependence on imported goods than before, but it also ushered in better times. The townspeople bought some wine, soap, and *piloncillo* (dried sugar cane) produced locally, but the supply was limited and irregular. For the most part, Laredoans relied on foreign and Mexican merchants from the interior for their flour, sugar cane, alcohol, and other articles of food and clothing. Not enough *arrieros* (teamsters) could be found to meet the demands for these imported goods. Artisans reappeared in town. Whereas in 1824 Laredo had listed only fourteen artisans, by 1828 it had thirty-two. Gaity and song returned as depression faded. On occasion the town became boisterous as it enjoyed its good fortune, and the *alcalde* suspended public dances temporarily.

Yet, while postrevolutionary times were an improvement over the war years, life in Laredo remained difficult. More Laredoans turned to farming as an occupation, but the production of

[32] The birthrates are crude estimates from extrapolated yearly population totals taken from the census returns for 1824, 1828 (Laredo Archives) and baptismal records at St. Augustine Catholic Church, Laredo.

maize in the area remained wholly inadequate. The number of farmers rose from thirty in 1824 to fifty-five in 1828, but the year's crop (122 *fanegas*, a dry measure approximately a bushel and a half) fell below the harvest garnered in good years (150 *fanegas*). To make up for this drop in production of maize, it was transported long distances to Laredo. Wool made this possible, and when the supply of wool fell, Laredoans resorted to the arduous task of hauling salt in order to exchange it for food and supplies from the interior.[33]

Leaders of the community maintained the school in operation through the 1820s and into the early 1830s. The exact effect of this educational effort is uncertain, however. Class was held year-round, but how many days per month or hours per day is not known. Nor is there information on attendance. Only one person was paid for teaching, and it is difficult to envision his holding class with as many students as the reports tell us were enrolled. Ironically, as the decade progressed, the school served a smaller proportion of the children of school age. In 1823 the average enrollment represented 50 percent of males aged eight to sixteen years; in 1828, it represented only 20 percent.[34] Nevertheless, the open door of the schoolhouse represented an achievement of the town and promise for the future.

The town's appearance remained unimpressive in spite of the new prosperity. Houses were evenly situated on rather long city blocks, and the streets were symmetrically laid out around two plazas. But most of the dwellings were *jacales*, and all had thatched roofs. The houses were small and meagerly furnished. Clouds of dust frequently hung over the streets. A lack of trees and shrubbery made the town appear desolate and stirred up in the minds of visitors images of oppressive summer heat even in mid-winter. The river water was murky and unsuitable for drink-

<hr>

[33] Data and notes in the censuses of 1824 and 1828, Rafael López de Oropeza, *bando*, 24 July 1826, records for the exportation of salt, April to November 1831, and Anastacio Bustamante to presidente municipal de Laredo, 17 March 1827, all in Laredo Archives. Also see José María Sánchez, "A Trip to Texas in 1828," *Southwestern Historical Quarterly* 29 (April, 1926): 251; Luis Berlandier and Rafael Chovel, *Diario de viaje de la comisión de límites que puso el gobierno de la república, bajo la dirección del exmo. sr. general de división d. Manuel de Mier y Terán*, p. 94.

[34] Monthly reports of the schoolmaster to the *cabildo*, in Laredo Archives.

ing without boiling. Laredo's only asset, according to those visiting the community with General Mier y Terán in 1828, was its strategic location on the Rio Grande on the road to Béxar.[35]

Debt continued to be a matter of importance to both rich and poor in Laredo. Wills in the postwar period record a number of large debts incurred among propertied Laredo families and to merchants and landowners in other towns and provinces. The estate of doña Juliána de la Garza Montemayor, for example, listed 5,786 pesos, 2 reales, in obligations along with the family's land and livestock. Indebtedness was also a problem for the impoverished. Some among the indebted poor fled Laredo rather than submit to a peonage system which amounted to slavery. The frequency of calls for assistance in returning runaways suggests both the widespread use of peonage and the extensive escape from it. Undoubtedly, continued migration in and out of Laredo encouraged exploitation of the transients and at the same time facilitated evasion of the harsher demands made by the creditors.[36]

By 1831 Laredo's population had decreased almost as rapidly as it had increased during the four years of relative prosperity. The population fell from 2,052 to 1,698. Reductions were experienced largely among the married aged seventeen to twenty-five years, at an average annual rate of 25.8 percent. The number of married individuals aged twenty-six to forty years fell, but at the much lower rate of 6.7 percent. Children under six years of age decreased by 7.5 percent and young men aged seventeen to twenty-five years, by 8.3 percent. The declines occurred almost in the same proportions by which these groups had risen earlier. Only the flow of older individuals and families into the town prevented the loss of population from being greater.[37] Who the migrants were and where they came from or went is unknown, but

[35] Berlandier and Chovel, *Diario de viaje*, pp. 93–94, 135; Sánchez, "Trip to Texas," p. 251.

[36] Will of Juliána de la Garza Montemayor, 25 February 1829, in Laredo Archives. See also wills of Petra Sánchez, 9 July 1822, Eugenio Hernández, 2 August 1825, María Gertrudes Gonzáles, 17 December 1826, and José Antonio García Dávila, 1828, also in Laredo Archives.

[37] Census of 1831, in Laredo Archives.

the census suggests that they were mostly young families with children. Prosperity in Laredo had proved illusory. Migrants discovered soon enough that available employment in sheep grazing and in the services created by the new wealth was limited. Without personal ties or economic stakes in the town, they left Laredo as swiftly as they had arrived.

Economic growth in the countryside undoubtedly drew many of those leaving the town to the far outskirts, where one *hacienda*, twenty-three *ranchos*, and one hundred *sitios* (parcels of common pastureland assigned to individuals) had been established within the last four years to accommodate the growing herds. The number of sheep had risen at an average rate of 25.9 percent annually since 1828. The number of horses had increased at about the same rate. These developments in the hinterlands may have absorbed the people who had been attracted to Laredo by the postwar prosperity but found the town's resources exhausted. Prosperity in the countryside eventually would encourage Indian raiding, but for the time being it provided employment for the poor and greater profits for the well-to-do.[38]

Owners of rural properties, all of them Laredo residents, benefited greatly from the economic growth in the countryside and consolidated their position of prominence in the town. Eighty-one individuals out of 559 adult males reported rural holdings. Within this group, distribution of land was very uneven. One-fourth of the land was owned by two individuals, and one-tenth by another two. The remaining land was divided in holdings of 500 pesos' worth or less. Conceivably, some of the large landowners were the patriarchs of extended families, in which case the distribution of land would not have been as uneven as it appears. By the same token, such an arrangement would have given these individuals considerable political power.[39]

Some of the landowners assumed the roles of merchants or

[38] Census of 1828, note in the census of 1831, in Laredo Archives.

[39] *Fincas rústicas*, or rural holdings, accounted for 85 percent of 21,214 pesos in property rendered; capital in drafts, 13.8 percent; and a miscellaneous category, 1.1 percent. Town properties were not taxed (Tax renditions to the state of Tamaulipas, 1833, in Laredo Archives).

moneylenders in order to profit from developments in trade. The census of 1833 reports the presence in Laredo, for the first time, of five resident merchants. They had expanded into commerce even though trade had suffered somewhat from the population movement away from the town. Growth in the countryside augured well for the merchants, and they and landowners supplemented the shortage in currency by issuing 2,900 pesos in drafts during the year 1833.[40]

A downward trend became noticeable in 1833 and was clearly evident by 1835. Reduced growth in sheep and goats and a small reduction in the number of horses between 1831 and 1833 turned into sizable declines between 1833 and 1835. A surprising increase in cattle during the first two-year period became a comparable decline by 1835. The census of 1835 records only half as much corn grown in Laredo as had been produced in 1833. The reduction of mules during the four years between 1831 and 1835 suggests a fall in the volume of trade, since mules were used in freighting. The census of 1835 also lists 6,834 pesos' worth of capital in drafts, twice as much as had been reported the previous year, suggesting that the town's economy became sluggish, currency became scarce, and the dependency on credit increased.[41]

The census of 1835 reveals indirectly that the racial and class divisions evidenced by the census returns between 1789 and 1821 persisted into the 1830s. The enumerator in 1835 saved and filed unofficial drafts of his returns in which heads of households were classed as *españoles*, *indios*, *mestizos*, or *castas*. Some *españoles* were accorded the title of *don*. Spaniards constituted one-third of the population in 1835, but of these only 20 percent, undoubtedly the small group of landowners, held the title of *don*. *Castas* made up the remaining two-thirds of the population. Thus, distinctions of race and rank in the community, first evident in 1789, had not disappeared by the mid-1830s, as the framers of the Constitution of 1824 had envisioned; on the contrary, they appear to have been hardened by war and economic chaos.[42]

At the root of the recession lay Laredo's inability to protect

[40] Occupational and wealth census of 1833, in Laredo Archives.
[41] Census of 1835, Laredo Archives.
[42] Unofficial draft of the census of 1835, in Laredo Archives.

itself from Indian raids or obtain assistance from the state government. Four muster rolls for a period between 1823 and 1827 list at least eighty volunteers in the Compañía Cívica de Laredo, and an observer notes that Laredoans took up military service as a hobby. But the efforts of the townspeople were insufficient to counter the raids. When requests for assistance went unanswered, the *alcalde* petitioned that Laredo be allowed to join the state of Nuevo León. Tamaulipas officials did not reply to this and may have considered the petition of secession merely a protest to their lack of concern.[43]

The Indian menace resurfaced in the early 1830s as state government, embroiled in the Conservative-Liberal struggle, became inoperative on the frontier. The *cabildo* in Laredo endorsed the revolts of Anastacio Bustamante and Antonio López de Santa Anna in hopes that these Centralists would assist the town and frontier in repelling Indian raids. Laredoans could not support the state officials in Ciudad Victoria who, unaffected by Indian attack and preoccupied with the control of customs revenue from Matamoros, had neglected the Rio Grande settlements for so long.[44]

Although the town's support for the Conservatives did not go beyond passing resolutions, the central government did take action against the Comanches and Lipan Apaches. These Indians, pushed south by Anglo-American settlement in Texas and other pressures, had renewed raids along the Rio Grande frontier and had made incursions deep into northern Mexico. In 1832 the national government sent an expedition to destroy Indian camps south and east of Laredo in Tamaulipas and Texas and north in Coahuila. The campaign, toward which Laredoans contributed horses, was deemed unsuccessful because of the lack of good scouts and the evasiveness of the nomadic Indians. The troops were frustrated and the officials disappointed, but the Comanches, whether because of the military campaigns or

[43] Records of the volunteer Compañía Cívica de Laredo for 4 December 1823, 6 June 1824, 1 September 1826, and 3 March 1827, and José Antonio Benavides to Antonio Elosúa, 3 July 1827, in Laredo Archives. See also Sánchez, "Trip to Texas," p. 251.

[44] Decrees of Nicolás Sánchez, comandante, and others, 28 January 1930, and of *alcalde* José Lázaro Benavides and others, 15 June 1833, in Laredo Archives.

for reasons of their own, stayed away from Laredo for a year or so, leaving the townspeople with the satisfaction that the national government had done something for them.[45] But by 1835 the raids had begun again.

Besides the Indian attacks, Laredoans suffered two bad epidemics. In 1831 small pox spread through the town, striking mostly the young and driving the mortality rate to 57.5 per thousand inhabitants.[46] Worse still, cholera swept through Laredo during the unusually hot summer of 1833. Of the 150 persons who died that year, 110 were victims of the epidemic. Most of them were small children. The death rate leaped to 87.1 per thousand, almost double the rate of the previous year. In the midst of dwindling economic resources, the cholera epidemic drained life and spirit from the community and left the townspeople helpless.[47]

In spite of epidemics and economic recession, Laredo's population increased between 1831 and 1835 from 1,698 to 1,978, almost up to the high mark of 1828. A large number of the immigrants were mature married men, apparently with larger and older families than those who had swarmed into the town during the boom years. The population would have been larger had not a sizable number of people left town, presumably to tend flocks in the countryside or find employment in other places.

Some of those moving to Laredo between 1831 and 1835 were associated with the return of the garrison to the town to counter the Indian raids. As before, the cost of such protection was high for Laredo in terms of disruption of the social order. The number of widows aged seventeen to forty years jumped from six in

---

[45] Report of Captain Manuel de la Fuente, 19 February 1832, in Laredo Archives.

[46] In 1829 and 1830 mortality rates were 31.6 and 41.1 per thousand. These and the crude death rate for 1831 are computed from extrapolated population figures and baptismal and burial records, St. Augustine Catholic Church, Laredo. At least 17.5 percent of the fatalities that year were caused by the epidemic, which killed fourteen small children six years of age and under and four adults sixteen years of age and over. These limited statistics are from the first quarterly report of vital statistics for 1831, Laredo Archives. The high percentage (73 percent) of deaths among children aged seven years and under is similar to that of the third quarterly report of vital statistics for 1830 (Laredo Archives), when the figure was 71.4 percent.

[47] Census of 1833 and vital statistics of 1833 and 1834, and Francisco V. Fernández to the *alcalde* of Laredo, 20 October 1833, in Laredo Archives.

1828 and eight in 1831, the years of peace and prosperity, to thirty-five in 1835. Among widowers and widows aged seventeen to twenty-six years, the disproportion between eight males and twenty females is glaring, especially in light of the fact that male and female death rates were very similar. The number of young widows and the presence of the garrison may have been alluded to in the remark of a *visitador* in 1828, who observed that Laredo damsels were particularly fond of military men and preferred their attentions to those of the more rustic local suitors.[48] Exaggerated and no doubt self-congratulatory, the observation nonetheless underscores the disruption caused by the presence of soldiers in Laredo.

The number of officers and men in the garrison, which fluctuated with the need for defense and the availability of state funds, affected in a large way enrollment and attendance at the town's school. During the periods when the troops were withdrawn enrollment fell by approximately a third. In September, 1829, for example, sixty-two students from the civilian population were registered and fifty from military families. Two years later, in July, 1831, seventy-six Laredo youths were signed up for the 1831–32 term, but only five children from the families in the garrison were registered. The financial support provided by the military for the school was important, but troop movements and the erratic pay schedule of the garrison disrupted the school program even as they disrupted the town's social structure.[49]

[48] Census of 1835, in Laredo Archives. Also see Sánchez, "A Trip to Texas," p. 251.
[49] School reports, 1 October 1829 and 1 August 1831, in Laredo Archives.

CHAPTER 3

The Border Moves South, 1835–50

Two major developments, which heretofore had seemed remote from life in Laredo, by 1835 began to unfold in the Mexican borderlands. The impact of the American westward movement was first felt in Laredo when Texans revolted against Mexico in 1835; less than a decade and a half later Laredo was included within the U.S. boundary as set by the Treaty of Guadalupe Hidalgo. In the midst of these difficulties Laredo was also caught in the political crossfire between Mexican Liberals and Conservatives. Already beset by a faltering economy and vexed by this internal and external disruption, Laredo entered into a period of depression.

The American Westward Movement

The presence of Anglo-Americans in the Mexican borderlands was not a recent phenomenon but one which had been developing for decades. Soon after American independence from England, settlers from the United States had broken through the geographic and economic barriers of the colonial period and by the turn of the century they were at Mexico's door. In the 1820s and 1830s, persuaded by the reports of traders, explorers, and filibusters, farmers trickled—and later poured—into East Texas. Both the United States and Mexico encouraged the westward movement along the southern coastal plains. The U.S. government had sponsored western exploration, purchased Louisiana, and provided land at generous prices. The Mexican Liberals, who controlled the national government after 1824, accepted and promoted American settlement in Texas as a way of reviving the economy of the borderlands and furthering the dominance of their political views, which they believed Americans shared with them.

But Mexican Liberals did not reckon with actual American

sentiments nor with the realities of the frontier. To Americans, their settlement of the Southwest appeared divinely ordained, and, given the expectations of the frontiersman and the military potential of the American government on the one hand and the sparse population and lack of substantial Mexican power in the borderlands on the other, American occupation of the area was indeed inevitable. Within a decade of the first settlement in Texas, Anglo-Americans outnumbered Mexicans there five to one. Simultaneously, Americans had migrated to the northern region of Mexican California and to the Pacific Northwest. The final step across the continent would come when President James K. Polk precipitated a war with Mexico by sending General Zachary Taylor to the banks of the Rio Grande opposite Matamoros.[1]

American invasion of Mexico and eventual occupation of Laredo seemed remote in the mid-thirties and early forties, however, when Laredoans faced the problems created by the Texas Revolution. Though far from the town, the troubles in Texas produced effects along the Rio Grande similar to those caused by the War of Independence. In organizing its military campaign against the Texas rebels, the Mexican government pulled the *presidio* troops from Laredo, and this action occasioned a new wave of Indian raiding. Other disturbances followed, two created by Texas, another by Mexican Federalists. Yet, for all the turmoil, Laredoans could not have foreseen the changes ushered in by the U.S. war with Mexico.

Most of the causes for the war lay distant from Laredo and the Rio Grande area. The American westward expansion in general and interest in California in particular rank as the principal causes for the war. Also important were the overconfident and belligerent attitudes in some political circles and in the press in Mexico City. In Washington, D.C., negotiations over the claims against Mexico broke down after the U.S. annexation of Texas. Likewise, President Polk's own political ambitions contributed to the outbreak of the war.[2]

---

[1]Ray Allen Billington, *The Far Western Frontier*, pp. 160–62; Eugene C. Barker, *Mexico and Texas, 1821–1835*, pp. 10–13.

[2]Seymour V. Connor and Odie B. Faulk, *North America Divided*, pp. 16–25,

Closer to Laredo was the American interest in the disputed territory between the Nueces and the Rio Grande. This facet of the westward movement was not related to the farmers' frontier but was inspired by commercial interests anxious to dominate the Mexican trade. By the early 1830s the trade between Saint Louis and Santa Fe and between New Orleans and Matamoros had flourished. Hopes of fully controlling both the overland and Gulf routes by acquiring jurisdiction over the two points of entry into northern Mexico helped inspire the Texas claim to the Rio Grande. Adding to the desirability of the Nueces Strip were huge herds of mustangs and wild cattle roaming the lower Rio Grande Valley. Texas traders had acquired, through legal and illegal means, large stocks of cattle from this area during the period of the republic.

Texas claims to the Rio Grande as the western and southern boundary of the state were never seriously considered by Mexican officials. Lands along the Rio Grande belonged to the states of Nuevo México, Coahuila, and Tamaulipas. Laredo was administratively bound to the latter, and all lands and *ejidos* on the east bank were adjudicated by the *cabildos* of Matamoros, Reynosa, Camargo, and Revilla. While the Nueces Strip was sparsely settled by Mexicans, no Texas settlements whatsoever existed there. Withdrawals of Mexican troops to points below the Rio Grande during the Texas Revolution did not constitute recognition of a boundary; these pullbacks were necessarily to the nearest garrison. Texan claims that Mexico had implicitly conceded the region were roundly rejected and disregarded by the Mexican government. Yet, despite the spurious nature of the Texas claim, it was this issue that brought hostilities between the United States and Mexico to the Rio Grande and resulted in the occupation of Laredo. At the conclusion of the war, Laredo, the single Mexican settlement of any size in the strip, found itself torn from the Mexican nation.[3]

27–32; Glenn W. Price, *Origins of the War with Mexico*, pp. 47–48, 91–93; John H. Shroeder, *Mr. Polk's War*, pp. 7–12, 51–53, 148–59.

[3] Billington, *Far Western Frontier*, pp. 25–27; LeRoy Graf, "The Economic History of the Lower Rio Grande Valley, 1820–1875" (Ph.D. diss., Harvard University), p. 58; D. W. Meinig, *Imperial Texas*, pp. 40–42. Also see Joseph M. Nance, *After San Jacinto: The Texas-Mexican Frontier, 1842.*

War and Depression

Changes in Laredo's economy in the middle 1830s reflected the cultural and political transformation of the entire Rio Grande borderland. As the number of immigrants from the United States grew in neighboring Texas during the 1820s, their presence in the Nueces Strip began to be occasionally evident to Laredoans. At first, contact was with travelers such as Stephen F. Austin, who journeyed through Laredo in 1822 on his way to Mexico City. Undoubtedly there were others of lesser fame, whether merchants, former filibusters, or drifters, whose passage through the town was not recorded. Actual references to Anglo-Americans in the 1820s appear only in the proceedings of the trial of two Mexicans charged with murdering Reuben Ross and in the report of the murder of David Price by an Irishman. There is also evidence of a lively trade in horses between Laredoans and Anglo-Americans in East Texas in the late 1830s and early 1840s. This trade made Texans and Laredoans aware of one another and, to some extent, interdependent.[4]

When the Texas Revolution came, the single event that directly touched the daily life of Laredoans was a confiscation of horses without due remuneration by Colonel Domingo de Ugartechea late in 1835. Military reports, requests for local assistance, and notices of troop movements related to the Texas Revolution remained unacknowledged by the *alcalde* in Laredo. Santa Anna's presence in northern Mexico drew the attention of the city fathers, not as an opportunity to express their support for the war against Texas but to press for assistance from the government in dealing with the Indian problem. In the winter of 1835–36, the threat of Indian attack had become a serious, frightening reality because the garrison was pulled away from Laredo to fight the rebels in Texas. Within a year's time twenty-six persons from the town were killed by Indians and over a thousand head of livestock stolen. Santa Anna neither replied to the request of the *cabildo* for aid nor sent reinforcements. All

[4] Seb S. Wilcox, "Laredo during the Texas Republic," *Southwestern Historical Quarterly* 42 (October, 1938): 88; trial records of Reyes Riojas and Ignacio Arispe, 30 May 1828, in Laredo Archives, St. Mary's University of San Antonio; Nance, *After San Jacinto*, p. 82.

contact with Indians created alarm, even the possibility that some peaceful Apaches under Cuelgas de Castro would settle near the town.[5]

The full implications of the Texas Revolution became clear to Laredoans in March, 1837, when Erasmus "Deaf" Smith, John C. Hays, and a party of twenty-two other Texans marched towards the town, intending to raise the flag of the Republic of Texas over the church steeple. The intruders were met at the Arroyo de Chacón five miles outside Laredo by cavalrymen from the *presidio*, and a battle ensued which left ten Mexican soldiers dead and several wounded. Shortly thereafter, when Smith became aware of the strength of the *presidio*, the Texans retreated to San Antonio leaving Laredoans apprehensive as they awaited the next move of their new enemy to the east.[6]

Refusing to accept the defeat at San Jacinto as decisive, Mexico immediately began preparations to reconquer Texas. Any assistance to the defenseless frontier towns was postponed indefinitely. The predictable results soon became evident. The number of sheep and goats held by Laredoans dropped from 5,800 in late 1835 to 1,500 in late 1837. The number of horses also dropped drastically in that two-year period from 548 to 100. The aggregate amount of capital in drafts fell from 6,834 to 3,000 pesos in that two-year interval, an average annual decline of 29 percent. By the same token, as Laredoans returned to planting the river bottomlands near the town, the production of maize rose by 22.5 percent, but the 1837 crop remained inadequate.

Depression ushered in dramatic population movements similar to those during the War of Independence. According to birth and death rates, Laredo's population should have risen by about fifteen persons in the two-year period between the census of 1835 and that of 1837. Instead, one of every eight persons in Laredo in 1835 had left, reducing the population from 1,979 to

---

[5]Open letter of Basilio Benavides to Santa Anna, 10 April 1836, printed in *El Mercurio del Puerto de Matamoros*, II, 67–68, n. 77, 22 April 1836, in Matamoros Archives, Barker Texas History Center, University of Texas, Austin; Juan José Flores to Idelfonso Ramón, 26 November 1835, report to the Governor, 7 March 1836, and Francisco V. Fernández to the *alcalde* of Laredo, 7 January 1836, in Laredo Archives.

[6]Nance, *After San Jacinto*, pp. 34–35; Wilcox, "Laredo during the Texas Republic," p. 98.

1,736, an average annual decline of 6.3 percent. The biggest losses occurred among married persons aged twenty-six to fifty years and among children aged eight to sixteen years. The number of individuals in these groups fell by 326 and 185 respectively, suggesting that numerous large, mature families were joining the exodus. That these families were replaced by younger ones is suggested by an increase of eighteen married males aged seventeen to twenty-five years and one of sixty-nine children aged seven years and under.

Other changes in population coincided with troop movements. These were of a character which must have affected friendships, courtships, law and order, and other relationships among Laredoans. Single males aged twenty-six to forty years rose from 17 persons in 1835 to 68 in 1837. Single females aged seventeen to twenty-five years rose from 39 persons to 132, and those aged twenty-six to forty years increased from 4 to 44.[7]

The school also was affected by depression and shifts of population. The schoolmaster held class through the spring of 1835, but under the pressing economic situation, closed the school during the summer. No reports are available for the remainder of 1835 or for the following year. In 1836 a school board was organized and a wider subscription for funds was undertaken to supplement the tuition paid by the parents. The teacher's salary did not improve, however, but fluctuated as before, from twelve to twenty-eight pesos monthly, depending apparently on the willingness or ability of Laredoans to fulfill their pledges.[8] The school closed again in 1837, when the depression worsened as the full effect of Texas independence was felt along the Rio Grande.

Besides disrupting the fragile equilibrium between the Mexican population and the Indians on the frontier, the Texas revolt and its aftermath may have indirectly undermined the relationship between Laredo and the Conservative Mexican national government. Besieged by requests for troops and frustrated by the difficulties in mustering resources for a new campaign against

---

[7] Censuses of 1835 and 1837, in Laredo Archives.

[8] Lista de ciudadanos que se comprometen a ayudar para el sueldo del maestro, 1837, in Laredo Archives.

Texas, General Vicente Filisola, the commander in Matamoros, expressed irritation over complaints by Laredoans of the inefficiency of *presidiarios* (soldiers). Laredoans, on the other hand, became disaffected with the national government, and although the *cabildo* had endorsed the Centralists as late as mid-1835, the *regidores* criticized the Mexican authorities for turning all their efforts to the Texas problem. One consequence of the government's neglect of the frontier was the recurring failure of the garrison payroll to arrive on time. This resulted in the *alcalde*'s personally advancing the money to pay the troops in order to prevent disorder.[9]

As the Indian raids increased in the late 1830s, the city council in Laredo shifted its support to the revolutionaries led by Antonio Canales, thus ending its traditional support of Loyalist and Conservative causes. On November 5, 1838, prompted by the success of the Texas Revolution, Canales's northern leaders had declared themselves in favor of the Constitution of 1824. Two months later, Laredoans, long the victims of neglect by Centralist state and national officials, sided with the Federalists. After a year of sporadic fighting, the Republic of the Rio Grande was created with Laredo as its capital. To what extent Laredoans participated in the rebellion is uncertain. One account suggests that Laredoans took an active part in some of the battles, but others refer only to the role of the garrison, which declared itself in favor of Canales but was defeated by Centralist forces in March, 1840. Three months later, a combined force of Texas volunteers and Mexican Federalists retook the town. Actually Laredo functioned as the capital only briefly. Guerrero, formerly Revilla, was the center of Federalist activity. Finally, in December, the civil war came to an end when Canales surrendered.[10]

When Canales's Federalist revolt was put down the Central-

[9] General Vicente Filisola to José María Ramón, 30 July 1837, resolution in support of the Centralist Republic, 22 June 1835, report of José María Ramón, 23 August 1838, Manuel Lafuente to Victor Vela, 4 June 1838 and 11 June 1838, and Esteban Telles to Victor Vela, 8 August 1838, all in Laredo Archives; *El Ancla*, 17 January 1840 (copy in Barker Texas History Center, University of Texas, Austin); Wilcox, "Laredo during the Texas Republic," p. 99.

[10] Charles Adam Gulick, Jr., and others, eds., *The Papers of Mirabeau Buonaparte Lamar*, III, 439, and VI, 128; Nance, *After San Jacinto*, pp. 253–60, 326–27.

ists left Laredoans to their own devices. Presidial forces did not put up a fight when John C. Hayes, who had been among the volunteers in the first Texan incursion, returned to Laredo with a force of Texas Rangers in January, 1841. This time the Texans came to punish Mexicans for alleged banditry which had broken out in the Nueces Strip. Both Mexicans and Texans had been engaged in rounding up stock on either side of the Nueces. Charges of theft had been exchanged by the two groups, and the Texas Rangers had made forays into the Nueces Strip in pursuit of bandits, although before 1841 no expedition had reached the Rio Grande. Finding the town practically defenseless, Hayes's party entered Laredo, gathered up horses, and pitched camp outside the town. The stock was returned the next day with the explanation that the seizure had been a show of force. Somewhat disappointed that a good battle had not taken place, the Rangers returned to Béxar.[11]

In the spring a company of Rangers under Hayes again approached Laredo. They suspected that Laredoans were harboring Agatón Quiñones, who had allegedly raided a cargo train from San Antonio. In a fierce engagement ten miles east of town the Rangers, armed with rifles, overpowered the presidial cavalry. Nine Mexicans were killed, three severely wounded, and twenty-five taken prisoner. Following the battle, the *alcalde* met the Texans at the entrance of Laredo and acceded to an investigation. The search did not turn up any bandits or evidence that Laredoans were involved in the raiding. The prisoners were then released and the Texans withdrew.[12]

On December 8, 1842, an army of 750 Texas volunteers, seeking revenge for General Woll's capture of San Antonio, passed through Laredo. Frustrated by the lack of adequate supplies, and perhaps giving vent to their hatred of Mexicans, some of the men plundered the town. Several cartfuls of booty were later returned by order of General Alexander Somerville, but

---

[11] Nance, *After San Jacinto*, pp. 46–47, 410; Gulick and others, *Papers of Lamar*, IV(1), 232–33, and VI, 116–17.

[12] Nance, *After San Jacinto*, pp. 410–13; Gulick and others, *Papers of Lamar*, IV(1), 233.

Laredoans claimed that goods worth 12,674 pesos were kept by the disorderly Texans.[13]

Besides Texans, Indians renewed their attacks on Laredo. When asked to mobilize the garrison to counter the raiding, the captain of the *presidio* explained to the *alcalde* that problems with ill-trained soldiers and desertions prevented him from taking effective action. The frustrated town leaders then recruited thirty-nine volunteers and launched a pursuit of hostile Indians along the Rio Grande above Laredo. Fortunately, the expedition, equipped with only seven horses and mules, two rifles, one bow, and one lance, did not encounter any bands, though it wounded two Indians before returning to the town. To assist settlers in other towns along the river to resist the *indios bárbaros*, Laredoans loaned them horses, which they never got back. Meanwhile, the national government excused its continued inaction by bemoaning the poor equipment of the army. By 1845 Indian raids, along with Federalist and Texan turmoil, clearly had taken its toll on Laredo. The town's population had increased by only 148 persons, a rate of less than 1 percent a year.[14]

American Occupation of Laredo

Laredo remained under Mexican administration for months after the war between the United States and Mexico began. General Taylor's advance was not through Laredo but along the well-established trade route to Monterrey via Camargo, Mier, and Cerralvo. The American flag was raised in Laredo for the first time by Texas volunteers under Captain Richard A. Gillespie, who passed through on their way to Camargo in July, 1846. In October an enterprising lieutenant from Taylor's army, Bryant Parrot Tilden, appeared in Laredo on a steamboat which he had sailed and dragged upriver to determine how far the Rio Grande

[13] List of claims for the raid of 1842, and petition submitted to the Texas legislature, 1850, in Laredo Archives.

[14] Policarpo Martínez to the *alcalde* of Laredo, 11 February 1842, report of Basilio Benavides to the *alcalde*, 11 February 1842, Francisco Pérez to the *alcalde* of Laredo, 12 February 1844, and census of 1845, in Laredo Archives.

was navigable. Finally, a month later, former Texas president "General" Mirabeau B. Lamar and a company of seventy-three men marched unopposed into Laredo to extend American jurisdiction over the town.[15]

The immediate effects of the war on Laredo were discernible in the early days of occupation. One of the first things Lamar ordered was an enumeration of the population by the Mexican authorities. It recorded 1,891 inhabitants, a net gain of 6 persons since the previous year. Raiding by Indians had continued to plague the outlying *ranchos*, and guerilla warfare with the invaders and banditry had cut the trade with the interior. After the initial impact, however, the large number of soldiers who had to be fed and supplied in the Rio Grande area became a bonanza for *rancheros* and farmers, who responded to the needs of the commissary and the quartermaster. Yet Laredo, outside the paths of the principal American forces invading Mexico, participated in the trade only marginally in comparison with other Rio Grande towns.[16]

The census of 1846 revealed that war, Indian troubles, and revolutions had changed the size of the household, just as they had affected other aspects of life in Laredo. The median number of individuals per household was 5.5, higher than that in the census of 1789 (4.0), the last enumeration which had recorded the size of the household. In 1789, slightly over half of the households contained four or fewer members, while in 1846 three-fourths of the households contained five or more. The smaller households in 1789 reflect the migration of families into Laredo during the initial period of settlement, while the larger households in 1846 attest to the migrations of single men and women which the censuses during and after the War of Independence recorded.[17]

[15] J. B. Wilkinson, *Laredo and the Rio Grande Frontier*, p. 200; Bryant Parrot Tilden, *Notes on the Upper Rio Grande*, pp. 1–2; Gulick and others, *Papers of Lamar*, IV(1), 141, and VI, 69–72.

[16] Gulick and others, *Papers of Lamar*, IV(1), 44–65, 179–81, and VI, 74–79; Graf, "Economic History," pp. 177–79.

[17] Unlike previous censuses, that of 1846 did not provide sex, age, and marital status information, but it did list all individuals in groups that appear to be households.

Despite internal problems related to discipline and fraud, Lamar's Guard provided Laredo with greater protection than the presidial force. One example of the Guard's efficiency was the quick pursuit of raiding Comanches and the recovery of a small boy taken by them during an incursion soon after the arrival of the Americans. Other than this, however, encounters with Indians were few, even though the soldiers spent much time scouring the country for Indians and Lamar described the potential danger as great. In time he and his volunteers came to consider the Laredo assignment as mere guard duty, and he repeatedly requested a more important command.[18]

American annexation of the Nueces Strip was a foregone conclusion as far as Lamar and other Americans in the area were concerned. Nueces County was created, and elections were held in the first month of the American occupation of Laredo. By annulling the Mexican wheel tax on merchants and by refusing to recognize the validity of indebted servitude, Lamar, as military governor, asserted the dominance of the new order. In the summer of 1847 he ordered elections for the city, and shortly thereafter disclaimed any American authority over the section of Laredo on the west bank. Months before the Treaty of Guadalupe Hidalgo was ratified, the Texas legislature created Webb County, embracing a large part of the Nueces Strip, and elections were held to select county officials.[19]

The creation of counties presented new opportunities to the Anglo-Americans already in the border areas to acquire public offices. In the first election, Lamar himself was chosen as the state representative from Nueces County. Later, one of Lamar's assistants, L. T. Tucker, was selected as justice of the peace. Tucker received more votes in the contest than did don Basilio

---

These groups are referred to as families, but the variety of surnames within most of the groups rules out the possibility that these are nuclear families.

[18] Gulick and others, *Papers of Lamar*, IV(1), 156–60, 162–63, 164–65, and VI, 69–72.

[19] Ibid., IV(1), 171, 186, 188; Wilkinson, *Laredo and the Rio Grande Frontier*, pp. 218–20. Texas governor J. P. Henderson had suggested a year earlier that Lamar organize the county as soon as possible (Gulick and others, *Papers of Lamar*, IV[1], 173–75).

Benavides, Lieutenant Colonel José María González, or don Francisco Villareal, all prominent Laredo men. After the creation of Webb County, James S. Wilkinson was elected county judge, and one of Lamar's lieutenants, Hamilton P. Bee, county clerk. The easy rise to public office of these newcomers in spite of the fact that most of the voters were Mexicans must have made the leaders of the old order apprehensive.[20]

The participation of native Laredoans in these elections was interpreted by Lamar as a sign that the initial hostility to the American occupation had dissipated. However that might be, Laredoans remained fearful of losing property rights. A petition of October 2, 1847, to the Texas state legislature requested assurance that land and inheritance rights would be upheld, peonage debts validated, *ejido* rights continued, and laws pertaining to the cattle industry left unchanged. The petition also asked that landowners not be taxed for the period when the Nueces Strip was in dispute, and that Laredo be granted lands to compensate for any public lands lost to the town because they were on the Mexican side of the river.[21]

Between the ratification of the treaty by the U.S. Senate (March, 1848) and its ratification by the Mexican Congress (May, 1848), the city fathers sent a petition to the American and Mexican authorities stating the wish of Laredo to remain a part of the Mexican Republic. The request came as a surprise to Lamar. It seemed incomprehensible to him that Laredoans could be ungrateful for the protection given by the army and for their political rights under the American system. Furthermore, he could not understand why Laredoans objected to American jurisdiction over an area which in his view had patently belonged to Texas since 1836. The appeal, sent to General Wood over Lamar's objections, cited lack of dependable protection against the Indians, the violation of property rights, and unacceptable American ways of dealing with wild stock as reasons why Laredo

---

[20] Gulick and others, *Papers of Lamar*, IV(1), 173, 184–85; Wilkinson, *Laredo and the Rio Grande Frontier*, p. 220.

[21] Gulick and others, *Papers of Lamar*, IV(1), 159–60; petition to the Texas legislators, Basilio Benavides in behalf of the citizens of Laredo, 2 October 1847, in Laredo Archives.

preferred to remain part of the Mexican nation.[22] But ratifications of the Treaty of Guadalupe Hidalgo were exchanged in Mexico City on May 30, 1848, and Laredo became a part of Texas and of the United States. By then Lamar and his volunteers had been mustered out of service, and Laredo was fully under civilian rule.

Laredo in 1850

At mid-century Laredoans east of the Rio Grande numbered only 1,173.[23] The apparent drastic drop in population occurred primarily because the former town was divided almost in half when the international boundary was set along the Rio Grande by the Treaty of Guadalupe Hidalgo.[24] Insecurity over the land question, the rapid social and political ascent of the Anglo-American newcomers, and the existence of family property on the Mexican side of the river led a number of additional Laredo families to resettle across from the town center in 1848. The population on the west bank then established the new town, which came to be known as Nuevo Laredo.[25] Other Laredoans left the town to settle in the hinterlands on the Texas side. During the same period, immigrants were coming into Laredo. The extent of the population changes is indicated by the fact that of all the residents enumerated in Lamar's census of 1846 only 261 were listed under the same names in the census of 1850. Al-

---

[22] José María Ramón and others to General John Ellis Wood, 10 April 1848 (referred to in Gulick and others, *Papers of Lamar*, IV(1), 197; and Wilkinson, *Laredo and the Rio Grande Frontier*, pp. 222–25); Gulick and others, *Papers of Lamar*, IV(1), 196–97.

[23] Statistics for this and the following paragraphs are compiled from manuscript returns of the United States Seventh Census, 1850, Schedule 1, Free Inhabitants, National Archives, Washington, D.C. (henceforth referred to as census of 1850).

[24] Octaviano Sosa, "Creación y denominación de la Villa de Nuevo Laredo," in *Centenario de Nuevo Laredo*. In 1846 Lt. Bryant P. Tilden estimated that a fourth of the town's population resided on the right bank; Lamar's estimate was higher, one-half (Tilden, *Notes on the Upper Rio Grande*, p. 2; Gulick and others, *Papers of Lamar*, VI, 59–72).

[25] Juan E. Richer, *Reseña histórica de Nuevo Laredo*, p. 516; Miguel Luna Rodríquez, *Reseña histórico-geográfica de Tamaulipas*, p. 29; Luis Benedicto, *Historia de Nuevo Laredo*, pp. 15–16.

though this figure may be deceptively low because of differences in the procedures of enumeration, the turnover appears sizable nonetheless.

A few bits of evidence suggest uneasiness among Laredoans over the relationship between Mexicans and Anglo-Americans as well as over land titles. Evidently fearful of Anglo-American displeasure, a group of leading citizens took up a subscription among themselves in 1849 to restore a rifle which had been stolen from an *americano*. In a similar manner they collected money to pay the expenses of an envoy to instruct the governor of Texas on landownership in Laredo. Later the city council paid for the translation of the *Acta de la visita de 1757*, the report of the inspection in which lands had been deeded to Laredoans.[26]

Any apprehensions and reservations about American rule were no doubt mitigated by the blessings of increased security. In 1849 the U.S. government had established Fort McIntosh as one of several army garrisons along the Rio Grande which would provide protection for the residents and prospective settlers in the river towns and fulfill the American commitment to control Indian depredations along the border.[27] The army took its obligation seriously and launched a vigorous campaign against the Comanches in the Nueces Strip. The effects were felt in Laredo when don Basilio Benavides's herd of horses was restored after a raid. *Vaqueros* returned to the *ranchos* in the now pacified countryside, and Laredo began a period of prosperity.[28]

The economic improvement is reflected in the increase of reported property values. In 1833, 21,214 pesos for rural property had been rendered, while in 1850 all real estate holdings were reported as being worth $212,500.[29] Although the 1833 tax

[26] List of subscribers to the fund for repayment of rifle stolen from the American, 1849, list of petitioners who own land on this side of the river, 1849, 5 February 1851, in Laredo Archives.

[27] Bill Tate, ed., *Guadalupe Hidalgo Treaty of Peace, 1848, and the Gadsden Treaty with Mexico, 1853*, pp. 21–23.

[28] Wilkinson, *Laredo and the Rio Grande Frontier*, pp. 227–28, 250–51; Jerry Don Thompson, *Sabers on the Rio Grande*, pp. 166–67.

[29] Census of 1833, in Laredo Archives, and census of 1850. Estimates vary on the value of the peso during this period. One of the best sources claims that as late as 1874 the peso was worth $1.04 (Diego G. López, *Historia del peso mexicano*).

records had not listed any town properties, this fact alone does not account for the rise in total property values. Either rural holdings were undervalued in 1833 or all properties rose in value when Laredo became part of the United States. Also, values reported in 1850 may represent holdings outside the Laredo area. In any case, the significant increase of real estate properties reported between 1833 and 1850 is indicative of stability provided by the new order.

The 104 persons reporting real estate holdings in 1850 constituted 39.2 percent, or two in five, of all the heads of households. The distribution appeared wider than in 1833, but real estate ownership, nevertheless, remained limited. Only 16.8 percent of all potential real estate owners (heads of households, persons listing an occupation, and all adults, excluding housewives) reported any holdings. Over half of the real estate still remained in the hands of a few, 15.3 percent. Each of three men, don José María González, don Juan José González, and don Bartolomé García, reported $10,000 or more in real estate. Added together, their holdings came to $32,000, or more than the total holdings of the forty-eight individuals in the three lowest categories. Among Anglo-Americans all but one of the seven heads of households reported real estate.[30] Three held over $5,000 in real estate. One of the three Irish immigrants reported $1,000 worth of real estate. In the short span of less than four years, non–Mexican Americans had acquired over 10 percent of the real estate reported by all Laredoans.

Among Anglo-Americans who reported occupations, four made up the merchant group in Laredo, two were clerks, two

[30] For the purpose of ethnic analysis, the population was divided into groups as follows: Mexican American, Spanish, Anglo-American, European, and black and *mulato*. The term Mexican American is of recent origin. In contemporary sources the terms Mexican, *mexicanos*, or sometimes *tejanos* were used to designate the inhabitants, citizens or not, of Mexican ancestry. Mexican American is the preferred term, however, because it distinguishes between those residing in the United States and those residing in Mexico. All persons of Spanish surname born in Texas or Mexico have been classed as Mexican American. Persons with Spanish surnames born in Spain are called Spaniards. Anglo-American refers to persons not of Spanish surname born in the United States, while European refers to persons not of Spanish surname born anywhere in Europe other than Spain.

filled the positions of chief justice (county judge) and sheriff, one was a carpenter, and three others were laborers. One of the three Irish immigrants worked as a merchant, one as a clerk, and one as a carpenter. One Spaniard was a "farmer" (in all likelihood he and the other "farmers" were stock graziers). Of the Mexican Americans reporting an occupation, 151, or slightly over half, were laborers; 20 percent were "farmers" (graziers); almost 20 percent worked in skilled trades—tailoring, making and repairing shoes or hats, and carpentry. There were also a priest, a teacher, a full-time "county officer," a weaver, and three blacksmiths. Not mentioned as gainfully employed were the fifty-two persons, presumably housewives, who contributed to family earning by offering services to boarders.

With respect to education, the 1850 census returns show that of the 381 children of Laredo aged six to seventeen years, half were reported as having "attended school within the year," a sizable number in comparison with previous years. All of the students except four were Mexican-American; the four were Anglo-American. Surprisingly, the proportion of school-age children attending classes was as high for girls as for boys. No correlation appears between school attendance and occupation, property holding, or size of family. Difficult to reconcile with the number of alleged students is the fact that only one person in Laredo reported his occupation as teacher, making the amount of instruction actually received by most of those who "attended school within the year" questionable. Yet past efforts to provide a teacher for Laredo's children, the 22.8 percent level of adult literacy, and the return of prosperity may well explain the apparent rise in educational effort.

The census of 1850 lists 264 nuclear families in Laredo. Of these, 153 consisted of two parents plus children, and 23 were childless couples, 17 of them married within the census year. One hundred and fourteen persons were not attached to nuclear families; 40 percent may have been related boarders, perhaps siblings. In over three-fourths of the households and in nearly two-thirds of the dwellings, nuclear families lived by themselves. Most of the remaining households and dwellings were inhabited by nuclear families plus boarders or other families.

A waterman hauling his load to Laredo homes, typical of both Mexican and American periods. *Courtesy Laredo Public Library.*

Women washing clothes in the Rio Grande. *Postcard, courtesy Laredo Public Library.*

Ruins in Nuevo Dolores, a nineteenth-century *ranchería* near the old *hacienda*. *From Yolanda Parker collection, courtesy University of Texas Institute of Texan Cultures.*

Ruins in Los Ojuelos, a nineteenth-century *ranchería* with many Laredo landowners. *Courtesy Laredo Public Library.*

Restored capitol of the short-lived Republic of the Rio Grande. *From Yolanda Parker collection, courtesy University of Texas Institute of Texan Cultures.*

Old Zapata County Courthouse, scene of a Civil War battle involving Laredoans. *Courtesy Laredo Public Library.*

Confederate Colonel Santos Benavides. *Courtesy Laredo Public Library.*

Left: General Manuel Mier y Terán, *visitador* in Laredo in 1828. *From Pemberton Press, courtesy University of Texas Institute of Texan Cultures. Right:* Raymond Martin, prominent local merchant who arrived in Laredo from France prior to the Civil War. *From* A Twentieth Century History of Southwest Texas, *courtesy University of Texas Institute of Texan Cultures.*

Confederate officers from Laredo, *(from left)* Refugio Benavides, Atanacio Vidaurri, Cristóbal Benavides, and John Z. Leyendecker. *Courtesy Laredo Public Library.*

Vendimias in the Laredo market, 1870s. *Courtesy University of Texas Institute of Texan Cultures.*

New stores on Iturbide Street, Laredo, 1875. *From Yolanda Parker collection, courtesy University of Texas Institute of Texan Cultures.*

Clothing and millinery store owned by European immigrants in Laredo. *Courtesy Laredo Public Library.*

St. Augustine Catholic Church, c. 1868. *From Yolanda Parker collection, courtesy University of Texas Institute of Texan Cultures.*

AYER

a las seis de la tarde fallecieron

en esta ciudad y en la FLOR de su edad,

El Club González-Guarache

y sus organos La Voz del Pueblo y La Geringa.

Mock obituary of the Guarache party, 1886. *From Yolanda Parker collection, courtesy University of Texas Institute of Texan Cultures.*

French priests in Laredo in the 1860s. *Courtesy Laredo Public Library.*

Very few single persons lived alone or as the heads of households or in dwellings in which boarders or others lived. Obviously, in spite of the vicissitudes of the 1830s and 1840s, the tradition of family life remained strong in Laredo.[31]

Nearly four-fifths, 202 of 257, of the nuclear families headed by Mexican Americans contained five or fewer members. Almost a fifth had six to eight members, and a handful had nine or more. The one Spanish family consisted of three members; the Irish family, five members; and the two Anglo-American families, two and three members. The enumerator recorded twenty dwellings inhabited by more than one household, and the possibility exists that these were extended family units. These multihousehold units are a very small percentage, 8.7, of all dwellings. The average (mean) number of persons per dwelling in 1850 (4.6) was lower than that in 1789, when seven persons lived in each dwelling. Thus, in 1850, the standard of living, at least regarding the number of people per dwelling, had improved.

Surprisingly, the drastic decline of the population in Laredo betwen 1845 and 1850 did not significantly alter the relationship between the various sex-age groups. Minor changes, such as the slightly larger decrease of younger children under eight years of age in relation to older children, may suggest the departure of more mature families. But the general stability of other groups (the highest losses were actually very small: twenty among males aged twenty-six to forty years, and twenty-nine among females aged seventeen to twenty-five years) may indicate that, despite all the changes which transpired in the second half of the 1840s, Laredo's social structure changed very little.

[31] The census grouped everyone according to census family (household) and dwelling. At times, two or more census families resided in the same dwelling, and less frequently members of one household resided in two separate dwellings. For the purposes of this study, "family" designates individuals who appear to be husband and wife, parent(s) and children, and in instances specifically defined, siblings. The census does not specify these relationships; they are inferred from names, ages, and the order of enumeration.

CHAPTER 4

The 1850s, A Decade of Change and Adjustment

Even before Mexican independence, New England peddlers sailing on sloops and steamers bound for Tampico and Vera Cruz had come ashore occasionally near the mouth of the Rio Grande or sold their wares to villagers along the Mexican coast. Eventually peddlers' goods began to be taken into the interior of Mexico on a trade route running from what became the port of Matamoros upriver to Camargo, one hundred miles below Laredo, then west to Monterrey, whence the goods were carried across the Sierra Madre. Once on the tablelands at Saltillo, the pack trains might veer north to Durango or as far south as Zacatecas, Aguascalientes, and San Luis Potosí. As a result of American access to the Mexican coastline from New Orleans, and because British competitors were distracted by the more lucrative Vera Cruz–Mexico City trade, Yankee merchants soon won control of most of the commerce through northeastern Mexico.[1]

Americans on the Border

About three hundred merchants, most of them from the United States, dominated the trade in Matamoros, a city of over four thousand inhabitants in 1834. The Americans were ousted during the conflict between Mexico and Texas, beginning in 1835, and the Europeans gained the upper hand. But many Americans

---

[1] Will of doña María Gertrudis de la Garza Falcón, in U.S. Congress, Senate, *Congressional Globe*, 35th Cong., 1st sess., no. 540, p. 962; George Folsom, *Mexico in 1842*, pp. 108–109; LeRoy Graf, "The Economic History of the Lower Rio Grande Valley, 1820–1875," (Ph.D. diss., Harvard University, 1942), p. 4.

returned to Mexico with the invading American army in 1846 and easily regained their previous dominant commercial position. When the Rio Grande was set as the international boundary after the war, most of the American merchants and many of the Europeans who lived in Matamoros moved to the American side of the river to the newly created town of Brownsville and established their stores and warehouses in order to conduct even more intensive trade with Mexico.[2]

In Brownsville, Anglo-Americans predominated numerically, economically, and socially. In 1850 they constituted slightly over half the population and held sway over the economy, filling 80 percent of the professional, mercantile, and government positions and owning all the town properties. Mexicans who had moved to Brownsville belonged for the most part to a propertyless lower class. They performed the menial tasks demanded by the mercantile economy, such as lifting and hauling, cleaning, and washing; they were water carriers, field hands, servants, and common laborers. Partly because of their economic power and partly because of their traditional attitude of superiority over Mexicans, the Anglo-Americans in Brownsville bore themselves somewhat haughtily. They had never intermarried with Mexicans in Matamoros and had seldom mixed with other foreigners there. Anglo-Americans looked down upon Mexicans, considering them lazy, given excessively to drinking, dancing, and gambling, and above all very docile and manageable.[3]

In Rio Grande Valley towns other than Matamoros-Brownsville the relationship between Mexican Americans and Anglo-Americans developed from a different initial experience, but the results were basically the same. Anglo-Americans who migrated to Laredo, Del Rio, Eagle Pass, and El Paso went in response to the demands for goods and services created by the various army

[2] Graf, "Economic History," pp. 48, 128–29, 153–55, 158; *American Flag*, 16 November 1846, 18 April and 18 December 1847. See also H. G. Ward, *Mexico in 1827*, I, 320–21.

[3] Census of 1850, National Archives, Washington, D.C. See also Eduard Ludecus, *Reise durch die Mexikanischen Provinzen Tamaulipas*, cited in Graf, "Economic History," p. 49; E. Domenech, *Missionary Adventures in Texas and Mexico*, p. 250; John Woodhouse Audubon, *Audubon's Western Journal, 1849–50*, p. 52.

forts established along the river. Once there, they expanded their businesses to include the trade with northern Mexico. These merchants were the founders of the border towns, with the exception of Laredo, and their enterprises stimulated the movements of settlers from the interior of Mexico to the Rio Grande. As economic and political leaders, Anglo-Americans quickly assumed positions and attitudes of superiority in all the river towns except Laredo.[4]

Because mercantile interests in the Rio Grande area had traditionally been handled largely by outsiders, Mexican Americans tended to accept Anglo-American control of trade, but American attempts to take possession of the land brought the two cultures into conflict. Under Spain and Mexico, *norteños* had valued the land for its grazing potential and used the profits from hides and wool to buy the food which the arid brush country could not produce. Given the sparse population, the land seemed abundant, with only the Indian menace and the dry, hot climate limiting the extent of its use. Legal ambiguities in the land titles were overlooked, and few conflicts arose, though boundaries were not clearly delineated, deeds were not held in common depository, and titles were encumbered by wills and deeds of sale. Since the issuance of the original grants the recipients, such as the settlers of Laredo in 1767, had begotten large families, whose claims to lands held in common ownership created a legal labyrinth. But as long as the patriarchs of the old Laredo families held control, few questioned the validity of the land titles.[5]

Anglo-American immigrants into South Texas brought concepts of landholding which upset the prevailing order. Though they used the land for grazing, not farming, they insisted on individual private ownership, surveys, the verification of all titles, and other legal requirements associated with the American agri-

---

[4]Louis J. Wortham, *A History of Texas*, V, 276; Walter Prescott Webb and H. Bailey Carroll, eds., *The Handbook of Texas*, I, 485–86, 532; C. L. Sonnichsen, *Pass of the North: Four Centuries on the Rio Grande*, pp. 119, 139–42.

[5]Florence Johnson Scott, *Historical Heritage of the Lower Rio Grande Valley*, pp. 64–68, 145–46; Scott, *Royal Land Grants North of the Rio Grande*, pp. 23–25; Graf, "Economic History," pp. 222–27.

cultural tradition. As merchants and lawyers, they possessed both capital and an acquaintance with the laws of Texas to help them acquire land. They demanded that the state create a commission to investigate and ascertain the validity of Spanish and Mexican land titles in South Texas. The procedure was complicated by the loss in a shipwreck of the report of the commission. A second investigation was conducted, and the report was accepted by the Texas legislature in the mid-1850s.[6]

Conflict over land use or ownership figured as the central issue or prominently in the background of the two major clashes between Anglo-Americans and Mexican Americans along the Rio Grande. The Cortina Revolt of 1859, triggered by the mistreatment of *mexicanos*, originated in Brownsville, an American-established town situated on the disputed Cavazos grant. As the conflict escalated, Juan Nepomuceno Cortina, the rebel leader, charged that loss of control of land left *mexicanos* defenseless. In El Paso the appropriation by a group of speculators of a previously public resource, the salt flats, resulted in a battle between the two ethnic groups.[7]

Besides the land-related issue, the Cortina Revolt and the Salt War reveal in several other ways the nature of the ethnic conflict. First, leadership among *mexicanos* came from the upper strata, which had been replaced by the Anglo-American newcomers: in Brownsville, from an established family which had lost land after 1848, and in El Paso, from the clergy, whose position in the community was challenged by the new economic and political leaders. Second, in both cases personal vendettas and unintended incidents obscured the original issue and ignited the emotions of those who supported or opposed the revolts, reflecting the lack of understanding on the part of the rebels of the full implications of the new order and the insecurity and ambition of the new leaders. Third, in both towns *mexicanos* may

---

[6] Scott, *Royal Land Grants*, pp. 26–27; Tom Lea, *The King Ranch*, I, 381; Robert K. Peter, "Texas: Annexation to Secession" (Ph.D. diss., University of Texas at Austin, 1977), pp. 162–63, 178.

[7] Proclamation of Juan Cortina, "Difficulties on the Southern Frontier," U.S. Congress, House, *House Executive Document*, no. 52, 36th Cong., 1st Sess., 1860, pp. 79–82; Final Report, "El Paso Troubles," *House Executive Document*, no. 93, 45th Cong., 2nd Sess., 1878, pp. 13–18.

have been reacting to a sense of powerlessness in the face of the overwhelming control of Anglo-Americans. Finally, the revolts were put down, but the pre-revolt harmony between the two ethnic groups, however fragile it may have been, was never regained.[8]

Because the conditions for armed conflict were absent, Laredo did not experience a clash along ethnic lines. Apprehensions over the validity of the original land grants disappeared when the legislature confirmed twenty land titles upon recommendation of a commission which had gathered evidence in Laredo in 1855. Other conditions of strife, such as rebel leadership among the upper strata of Mexicans, clearly drawn sides, and complete control by the Anglo newcomers, were not evident in Laredo. Conflict between the leaders of the old order and the challengers of the new and between two different traditions of land, social order, and legal customs could not be submerged completely, to be sure. But the complex relationship that developed between Anglo-Americans and Mexican Americans was often mutually beneficial and never outwardly hostile. In Laredo the coalitions that evolved were not principally ethnic; instead, they pitted the privileged, whether Anglo, European, or Mexican, against the poor.[9]

[8] Both events have elicited considerable historical coverage. Cortina has been portrayed as the typical bandit in popular works such as Walter Prescott Webb's *The Texas Rangers*, pp. 175–83, and Lynn Woodman's *Cortina: The Rogue of the Rio Grande*, p. 8. Others such as Charles W. Goldfinch, *Juan N. Cortina, 1824–1892: A Re-Appraisal*, pp. 39–40, 46–47, point to class resentment as the basis for the revolt and stress Cortina's own concern for legality and propriety as an argument against the "bandit" label. Rodolfo Acuña in *Occupied America*, pp. 46–47, attempts to describe the revolt in accordance with the "social bandit" model presented in E. J. Hobsbawm, *Primitive Rebels: Studies in Archaic Forms of Social Movement in the 19th and 20th Centuries*, pp. 110–12. Graf, in "Economic History," pp. 375–81, describes how the revolt began as a personal vendetta against individuals who had abused Mexicans in a visible and violent manner.

Like the Cortina incident, the Salt War lends itself to various interpretations. Seymour V. Connor in *Texas: A History*, pp. 234–35, treats the incident as part of the lawlessness of the Reconstruction period. C. L. Sonnichsen in *The El Paso Salt War, 1877*, pp. 19–20, recognizes the clash of traditions as the basis for the incident, even as he describes the particular individuals and unique events that set the fuse afire.

[9] Scott, *Royal Land Grants*, pp. 26–27; Jerry Don Thompson, *Sabers on the Rio Grande*, p. 161.

Adjustment in Laredo

The most evident symbol of the new era in Laredo was the presence of American troops. The number of soldiers assigned to Fort McIntosh varied during the pre–Civil War period from the single company which arrived in Laredo eight months after the departure of Lamar's Guard to 432 men in eight companies in 1853. Later, on the eve of the Civil War, military strength was reduced to a single unit of 82 soldiers. The effectiveness of the troops as protection against Indians was limited at times by the lack of mounts, as was the case in 1853 when the garrison had only thirty horses. When Texas Rangers were sent into the Laredo area, the Rangers and the army each blamed the other for failure to prevent Comanches and Lipan Apaches from raiding the countryside with impunity. In early 1854, the citizens of Laredo petitioned the governor of Texas for better protection, lamenting the town's losses in life and property and demanding the extermination of the entire Lipan Apache tribe. But the soldiers, having gained experience on the frontier, improved their fighting skills, and the Indians turned south and attacked less adequately defended villages on the Mexican side of the river.[10]

In the last years of the decade, however, the Apaches renewed their raids on the outlying *ranchos*, and Laredoans were forced to rely on their own resources to meet this threat because of the reductions in the force stationed at Fort McIntosh. When the raids began, some Laredoans, complaining of army inefficiency, requested the replacement of the cavalry with another outfit; instead troops were withdrawn. An eighteen-man brigade was then organized under don Refugio Benavides, but it is uncertain whether the Apaches eluded this unit or whether the volunteers never marched out in pursuit of the Indians.[11]

Even when ineffective against continued Indian raiding,

---

[10] Post returns, Fort McIntosh, Laredo, Texas, records of the Adjutant General's Office, record group 393; National Archives, Washington, D.C. Also see Thompson, *Sabers on the Rio Grande*, pp. 165, 176–78; Stephen B. Oates, ed., *"Rip" Ford's Texas by John Salmon Ford*, pp. 171–81, 189.

[11] Entry for 11 September 1859, Minute Book, II, Laredo city records, Office of the City Clerk; J. B. Wilkinson, *Laredo and the Rio Grande Frontier*, p. 271.

the large military force in Laredo constituted a market for property, goods, and services. The federal government at first leased the *ejidos* on which the fort was situated. Later it bought the land as well as properties with *casas de campo* (ranch houses) near the fort owned by individual Laredoans. Food for the men and fodder for the animals was acquired locally, guides and interpreters from the community were hired, and the soldiers no doubt spent some of their pay in Laredo.[12]

As in earlier periods, the presence of a garrison in Laredo and a stream of new immigrants to the town created difficulties in the regulation of public order. The aldermen passed a resolution in 1850 requiring strangers to register with city authorities, and in 1854 some town leaders proposed that a vigilante committee divide the town into sections and patrol the streets in search of vagrants.[13] When the problem appeared again in 1858, a commission was formed to incarcerate all strangers until their honesty could be ascertained. In 1859 the Board of Aldermen in an attempt to uphold law and order passed a series of resolutions that placed a curfew on saloons; forbade the wearing of guns in public; controlled the discharge of firearms within the town limits; regulated the speed of carriages and horses on the streets; required licenses for billiards, *fandangos* (public dances), and other entertainments; prohibited obscene language and indecent acts in public; and restricted the bathing areas along the river.[14]

Sharp divisions among the townspeople along ethnic lines seem to have been avoided. Interaction between Mexican Americans and Anglo-Americans was to a great extent characterized by cooperation, blending, and mixing. Gestures toward getting

[12] For the agreement between Laredo and the U.S. government on the property of Fort McIntosh see the entry for 19 March 1859 in Minute Book, II, Laredo city records. For the arrangement on the purchase of houses, see entries for 16 and 17 July 1859, 10 and 25 July 1860, and 7 September 1860. Also see Thompson, *Sabers on the Rio Grande*, pp. 175–76.

[13] Resolutions of 29 June 1850 and 24 June 1854, City Ordinances, Laredo Archives, Barker Texas History Center, University of Texas, Austin.

[14] Ordinances of 4 September 1858 and 1 March 1858, and resolution on vagrants and thieves, 29 May 1859, Minute Book, II, and Ordinances of 8 January 1859, 27 July 1860, City Ordinances, II, 6–7, 15, Office of the City Clerk, City records, Laredo.

along included the publication of ordinances in both English and Spanish, celebration of American and Mexican national holidays, and division of political offices more or less equally. Anglo-Americans and Europeans in Laredo, according to local tradition, learned Spanish, mixed socially with the Mexican-American upper class, and intermarried with them. They often appeared more Mexicanized than *mexicanos* appeared Americanized.[15]

Yet, in spite of social amiability among Laredoans of all groups, some ethnic distinctions were unavoidable, especially in politics. In keeping with their respective expectations and with the pattern established initially, Anglo-Americans dominated county government in the early fifties, while Mexican Americans controlled the Board of Aldermen. In 1852 three Anglo-Americans and a British immigrant did capture four of the six seats on the Board of Aldermen, but in the following year Mexican Americans retook all the positions and held them until 1857, when Garner W. Pierce was elected to the board. Pierce was an active member, introducing several resolutions and making nominations for appointive positions. Mexican Americans remained in control of city government, nonetheless. Toward the end of the decade they took over the county government as well.[16]

Occasionally the actions of the Board of Aldermen reflected the broad economic interests of ethnic groups in Laredo. In general, Mexican Americans farmed and ranched while Anglo-Americans were merchants. In the early part of the 1850s, under Mexican-American administration, the aldermen clarified Laredo's rights over the *ejidos* and the process by which the land could be used by the townspeople. The Anglo-American—

[15] Hamilton P. Bee to Santos Benavides, 9 November 1863, and Santos Benavides to Hamilton P. Bee, 12 November 1863, in *War of the Rebellion: A Compilation of the Official Records of the Union and Confederate Armies*, series I, XXVI(1), 409, and XXVI(2), 398–99; *Corpus Christi Ranchero*, 21 January 1864 (copy in Barker Texas History Center, University of Texas, Austin).

[16] Minutes of city board of aldermen, 2 January 1851, 1 and 28 January, 10 and 23 April 1852, 26 December 1853, 25 June 1854, 23 April 1855, 17 and 18 July, 4 January 1856, 28 April 1857, Minute Book I, and 8 August and 15 December 1857, 4 and 16 January, 17 February, 24 August, 1 September, 13 December 1858, 3 January and 12 December 1859, 20 January, 25 and 26 June 1860, Minute Book, II, City records, Laredo.

dominated board, on the other hand, in 1852 introduced measures restricting the use of the commons. When Mexican Americans returned to power the following year, the restrictions were eased. By the same token, antimerchant traditions among Mexican Americans may have influenced the passage of a store tax in the early 1850s.[17]

Whatever economic and political polarization existed between the two ethnic groups in the early years, it disappeared as new economic realignments emerged. Some of the *ejidos* were surveyed and laid out in town lots, which were then put up for sale by the city, an action which resembled town promotion schemes along the American frontier.[18] Mexican Americans with savings and capital moved into merchandizing, setting up stores in different parts of town, booths in the plaza, and even shops in their homes. The board voted city funds for public improvements requested by the business community. These included garbage pickup, street sweeping and repair, improvement of access to the river, and the erection of a market. Wealthier merchants came to exercise considerable influence on the board and prevented the repeal of the store tax, which in the late fifties was used to limit competition from smaller retailers.[19]

At the courthouse, top county officials were initially all Anglo-American, but Mexican Americans were represented adequately in some positions and on the juries in the district court. Three grand juries met during the fifties. On one, all the jurors were Mexican Americans; on the other two, the foremen and

[17] Resolutions on the use of the *ejidos*, 11 March, 1 June, and 26 July 1851, *Libro de Acuerdos de la Ciudad* and 12 January, 2 and 24 February 1852, Minute Book, II (see also Registro de Solares), City records, Laredo; fees paid for the use of *ejidos*, January to December 1855, Laredo Archives, Austin.

[18] Resolution for a committee to draft ordinance governing the sale of *ejidos*, 23 May 1857, and sale of *ejido*, 2 May 1859, Deed Book, January 1859–June 1888, City records, Laredo.

[19] Resolution to create a committee to draft an ordinance, 12 January 1852, Minute Book, I, and proposed ordinances on taxing small business establishments, 3 March 1859, petition to exempt small businesses from the store tax, 23 June 1859, report on the completion of the market, 26 December 1859, Minute Book, II, City records, Laredo; petition of citizens requesting the city to repair streets, 10 February 1858, plans for a public building, 4 May 1855, transcripts, Laredo Archives, St. Mary's University of San Antonio; bids for market building, December 1858, and reports on repair of streets and access to the river, 15 and 23 August 1859, in Minute Book, II, Laredo Archives, Austin.

two jurors were Anglo-Americans. Twelve petit juries were chosen. Three were entirely Mexican American. On the other nine juries, ten or eleven members were Mexican Americans, but six of the nine juries chose an Anglo-American as foreman. The preference for Anglos as foremen is perhaps attributable to their command of the English language or their acquaintance with the Texas legal system.[20]

Only seven criminal cases were tried in Laredo during the 1850s. Charges were aggravated assault (two cases), burglary, larceny, malfeasance in office, cattle stealing, and selling liquor without a license. All cases save one had some Anglo-American jurors. Of the individuals tried, only two appear as residents of Laredo in the census returns of 1850 or 1860. All were Mexican Americans except the one charged with selling liquor without a license. Justice of the Peace Albino Treviño was found guilty of malfeasance in office, but the sentence was suspended because of his ignorance of the legal system. The most sensational trial must have been that of don Basilio Benavides, who was charged with aggravated assault. He was found guilty, but the conviction is not known to have affected the reputation of the sixty-year-old patriarch of his family.[21]

Seven civil suits were brought before the district court. Four of these suits were for debt, one concerned a land title, another was over a contested election, and one for divorce. Understandably, all but the last involved persons of some standing in the community. Three Mexicans and five Europeans were naturalized as American citizens during the same time, perhaps a sign of confidence in Laredo's future within the United States.[22]

Laredo's American experience appeared beneficial to the town, at least economically. The army, besides furnishing protection for graziers, provided security for trade with northern Mexico, thus permitting the fulfillment of the long-standing prediction that Laredo's best asset would prove to be its good loca-

[20] Minutes of District Court, I, 1–3, 6–10, 16–22, 24–25, 29–32, 36, 47–53, Webb County Records, Office of the District Clerk, Laredo.
[21] 28 April 1857, Minute Book, II, City records, Laredo.
[22] Minutes of District Court, I, 2, 4, 12–14, 17–18, 34, 37–39, 46, Webb County Records, Office of the District Clerk, Laredo.

tion as a river crossing to the interior of Mexico. In the mid-fifties Laredo and Eagle Pass together enjoyed over $500,000 annually in trade. In Laredo five large stores, a handsome new courthouse, a new market building, and a convent under construction attested to the material well-being of the town. The intermittent noise from the stones at the mill grinding wheat and corn for the townspeople signified better times. Two lots were donated by the city for a school, and José María Rodríguez, who later played an important role in county politics, was hired as the teacher. A setback in trade in the last years of the decade was disappointing to one observer, but it seemed to him that Laredoans viewed it as temporary.[23]

Laredo in 1860

By 1860 Laredo's population had increased to 1,306 from 1,173 in 1850, a gain of only 243 persons, or an average annual growth of 1.1 percent. Accompanying this miniscule growth was a sizable turnover of the town's population. Of all those enumerated in the 1850 census, only 186 were listed in 1860. Church records for the decade further demonstrate the extent of the change in the town's population. Although 1,020 infants were baptized during the 1850s, only 411 children, ten years of age and under, were counted in the 1860 census. During the decade, the pastor presided at 400 burials, a figure which cannot alone account for the many individuals who no longer lived in Laredo by the end of the period.[24]

While the population movement during the decade did not alter the size of households or dwellings, it did affect their structure. The average (mean) dwelling in 1860 still housed 4.6 persons, and the average household still held 4.4 individuals, but changes occurred in the types of dwellings and households.

[23] For a description of Laredo by an unidentified observer, see *Texas Almanac, 1859*, p. 185. Also see Wilkinson, *Laredo on the Rio Grande*, pp. 271, 276.

[24] Baptismal records, St. Augustine Catholic Church, Laredo. Statistics in this and the following paragraphs are compiled from the census of 1850 and the Manuscript Returns of the United States Eighth Census, 1860, Schedule 1, Free Inhabitants, National Archives, Washington, D.C.

While the number of households rose from 265 to 280, an increase of 5.6 percent, with the growth in population during the fifties, households made up of single individuals multiplied sixfold, from 6 to 35. Households headed by single persons plus a family and boarders increased from 5 to 17. Households composed of nuclear families by themselves decreased from 207 to 164, a drop of 22.2 percent.

The changes in the makeup of the dwelling were similar in some respects and different in others. While the number of dwellings rose from 233 to 268, an increase of 15 percent, dwellings housing single individuals increased fifteenfold, from 2 to 32. Those inhabited by single individuals plus a family and boarders increased from 4 to 23. The number of dwellings inhabited by nuclear families by themselves in 1850, 149, rose by only one in 1860. Multiple-family dwellings, however, decreased from 78 to 63. The most salient change in dwelling size was the 8.9 percent increase in the number of dwellings inhabited by one person.

Changes in the population and economy of Laredo appear not to have affected the nature of the family, at least outwardly. Ninety-one percent of all Laredoans (1,190 individuals) were listed as belonging to a nuclear family. Of the remaining 9 percent, close to half had the same last name as some of the other members of the household and were probably related to them. Among all families, the proportion of childless couples and families with both parents living remained basically the same in 1850 and in 1860. The proportion of families headed by single parents likewise remained the same in both censuses, but within this group families headed by women rose slightly (5 percent) during the decade. Perhaps attributable to the military contingent in the town were the large numbers of washerwomen (thirty-six) and seamstresses (fifty-three); their presence in 1860 stands in contrast to their absence at the time of the previous census. The size of families likewise remained practically the same. Three-fourths of all families contained five or fewer members. Only a tenth of the families contained eight or more persons.

In spite of the movement of people through Laredo, the

age-sex ratios within the community in 1860 remained remarkably similar to those of ten years before. The dependent segment of the population, youths aged sixteen years or less, made up the same proportion of Laredoans (about half) as a decade before. This ratio is not significantly changed if adults aged fifty-one years or more are included as "dependent." The ages of workers likewise did not change. Seven-tenths of the semi-skilled and unskilled male laborers, for example, were, as usual, between sixteen and thirty-five years of age. Among females, the range was somewhat lower, between twelve and thirty-one years of age. the most salient difference between the two decennial enumerations was the doubling of the number of women aged fifty-one years and over.

One clear sign of Laredo's transformation was the increasing variety of occupations. The town had gained a lawyer, a doctor, a surveyor, a dozen more merchants, a half-dozen more clerks, one post trader, a baker, a gunsmith, a machinist, and three wheelwrights. The number of masons increased by five, perhaps because of the need to repair the old buildings and erect the market, the convent, and the new homes and stores. Losses and replacements in other occupations likewise reflect changes in the economy. In 1850, the census listed seven carpenters, three blacksmiths, one blacksmith apprentice, fifteen tailors, and three silversmiths; a decade later the census listed only six carpenters, one blacksmith, four tailors, and no silversmith or blacksmith apprentice. With the increase in the number of single individuals living by themselves and heading households and dwellings, additional positions opened for twenty-seven cooks, sixteen housekeepers, and forty-eight servants. The number of common laborers remained about the same, but they now constituted only 26 percent of the work force as against 52 percent in 1850. Only twenty-seven persons were listed as stock raisers in 1860, half as many as in 1850, indicating clearly that Laredo had taken a step away from a pastoral economy toward a more diversified commercial one.

Although the number of persons reporting real estate remained constant (106 in 1850, 107 in 1860), the total reported value of real estate fell from $212,500 to $78,572. The number of individuals reporting real estate values under $500 increased from 6 to 58, while those reporting values $500 and above dropped from 98 to 49. The dramatic change may have been occasioned by an exodus of wealthier Laredoans to the outlying *ranchos*. But, when allowance is made for the drastically lower valuations in 1860, the distribution of owners into the general categories of small, medium, large, and very large remains strikingly similar.

The appearance of Raymond Martin, an immigrant to Laredo from France, among the three wealthiest property owners in 1850 is indicative of change in leadership in the town. Yet the relationship between rich and poor remained about the same. Martin and nine other Laredoans reporting properties valued $2,500 and over owned half of all the wealth in real estate, more than the eighty-two individuals reporting properties valued at less than $1,000. Fourteen others reported real estate holdings valued from $1,000 to $2,000; together they owned 36.2 percent of the aggregate value of real estate listed in the census. These twenty-four persons composed only 5.6 percent of Laredo's potential real estate owners (428 individuals).

Whereas only 107 persons in Laredo reported real estate, a total of 249, nearly 60 percent of the single adults and heads of households and families, reported personal estate. The aggregate value of these personal estates was $126,194. One hundred and sixty-two of the 249 personal estates were worth less than $250 each and totaled only 12.7 percent of the value of all personal estates. Seventy-one other persons listed personal properties appraised between $250 and $1,000. Added together, holdings of less than $1,000 accounted for only a third of all personal wealth. Another third was held in personal estates valued at $1,000 to $5,000. The final third was accounted for by five men: Santos Benavides, Alphonse Martin, and Charles Callaghan, $5,000 each; John Rigos, $8,000; and Raymond Martin, $22,000. The concentration of wealth in personal estate was thus comparable to that in real estate.

In spite of the economic transformation of the town during the 1850s, few strides were made in education. If the enumerators are to be trusted, adult illiteracy rose from two-thirds of the population in 1850 to three-fourths in 1860. Of the illiterate, well over half were women; 78.6 percent of the illiterate males reported unskilled occupations or no occupation. Among 350 children of school age, only 48 attended school in 1860, over half of whom were girls. The proportion of children attending school in 1860 (13.7 percent) was considerably smaller than in 1850 (approximately half), but this may be attributed to different definitions of "attending school within the year."

Half of the Mexican-American population in 1860 still worked in unskilled positions as common laborers, servants, washerwomen, and shepherds. The number of semiskilled workers had risen, but the appearance of upward mobility was probably more illusory than real, for positions such as cook and seamstress, though requiring some skills, were not well remunerated or held in much esteem. Cartmen, of whom fifty-eight were listed in 1860, enjoy a special place in Mexican folklore, and some of the cartmen in Laredo may have been former *vaqueros*, shepherds, or common laborers who were taking advantage of opportunities offered by the growing trade with northern Mexico to move up to a better occupation.

Among Mexican Americans, who made up 97 percent of Laredo's population, many were recently arrived immigrants born on the Mexican side of the Rio Grande. In 1850 the Mexican-born composed only 1.9 percent of the Mexican Americans in Laredo, but in 1860 they had risen to a fourth. They resembled Texas-born Mexican Americans in their family status. Eight of ten belonged to a nuclear family, and about half of the remainder bore the same surname as someone else within the household. In their occupations the Mexican-born also resembled the entire Mexican-American group. Among the Mexican-born were two merchants, one clerk, a scattering of craftsmen, six cooks, six cartmen, ten seamstresses, and eighty-eight laborers, servants, and washerwomen. Their illiteracy rate was higher by 18 percent than that of all Mexican Americans. Their holdings of real and personal estate were proportionately smaller than the holdings of all Mexican Americans, but by no means insignificant. All told, Mexican Americans born in Mexico possessed a total of $17,000 in personal estate and $10,560 in real estate, approximately 13 percent of all the wealth reported by Laredoans in these categories. Compared with all Mexican Americans in Laredo, they fared rather well and in some respects, one being the proportion of their children attending school, they fared even better.

Twenty-one Anglo-Americans resided in Laredo in 1860, as against twenty-eight in 1850. Three of them were born in New England, ten in southern and border states, and eight in Texas. Seven of the Anglo-Americans were aged sixteen years or under; two, seventeen to twenty-five years; eight, twenty-six to forty years; two, in their forties; and two, over fifty-one years. All but two were males. One of the seven children was born of a mixed marriage, and another was cared for by an apparently unrelated adult. The lone two-parent family had five children, four boys and one girl. The twelve remaining Anglo-Americans were all adult males, four of them apparently brothers. The occupations of the adult males were a lawyer, a doctor, a surveyor, a book-keeper, a post trader, a carpenter, a wheelwright, two clerks, and five merchants. Five of the Anglo-Americans reported real estate totaling $8,200 and personal estate totaling $16,550— about one-tenth of the total real estate and one-eighth of the total personal estate reported in Laredo. It seems from the proximity of their listings in the census returns that most of the Anglo-Americans lived near one another in the center of Laredo, either close to or behind their stores.

There were also eleven Europeans in the community, six from France, four from Ireland, and one from Germany. The German had come to Laredo via the German settlement in central Texas. Three of the Europeans were merchants, one was a gunsmith, one a baker, and one a laborer. Two French priests had replaced don Trinidad García after the parish of Laredo came under the jurisdiction of an American bishop. One of the Europeans was the head of a family in which the spouse and children bore Spanish first names. The others were single males, mostly aged twenty-six to forty years. The combined personal estate of six of them totaled $27,850, or over a fifth of all personal property held in Laredo. Three reported real estate, their total holdings valued at $12,700, approximately a sixth of the Laredo

total. Most of the European immigrants lived near the center
of town, close to the *americanos* and the well-to-do Mexican
Americans.

Local tradition maintains that the Europeans got along better with the Mexican population and formed closer bonds with
them than did the Anglo-Americans. The Europeans, nevertheless, shared many interests with Anglo-Americans. Both groups
were newcomers with capital and commercial ties beyond Laredo. Their prosperity, at least initially, did not depend on the
traditional economic resources of Laredo, and their success was
not bound to the well-being of the community. Together with
the Anglo-Americans they controlled approximately a fourth of
the land and a third of the wealth in personal estates. Obviously,
both immigrant groups influenced substantially the economic
and social life of Laredo.

Only 186 of the persons enumerated in Laredo in 1860 were
present in the town when the census of 1850 was taken. Surprisingly, this small group of "persisters" and the large contingent of newcomers were strikingly similar in age, sex, occupation, family status, and ownership of real estate. The two groups
differed significantly only in the proportion of foreign-born and
the distribution of personal estates. Proportionately there were
more Mexican-born individuals (25.2 percent) among the new
population than among the persisters (13.4 percent). Among
those persons reporting personal estates, wealth was somewhat
less evenly distributed in the new group than in the old. These
differences point to the migration of many poor Mexican-born
individuals into Laredo during the 1850s. Yet a similarity of occupational levels and real estate holdings between the new population and the persisters and the fact that three newcomers and
only one persister reported personal estates over $5,000 suggest
that not all the newcomers were poor. Approximately 30 percent
of the persisters and only 15 percent of the new population reported amounts above $500.

CHAPTER 5

The Civil War and Reconstruction

Texas' geographical size and heterogeneous population, creating a variety of economic and social interests, made unanimous support for the Confederacy difficult. Its secession from the Union, coming not long after a vigorous campaign for annexation, is somewhat perplexing. States' rights, sectionalism, and abolitionism all contributed to the secession controversy, but these issues do not fully explain how Texans from diverse backgrounds, some living in isolated regions, were drawn into the national conflict. Perhaps the personal political commitments of minor state and local figures to more prominent officials and planters who favored secession may have been the central force in the overwhelming approval of the secession ordinance.[1]

The far-reaching causes for secession do not appear to have influenced Laredo's vote on secession. Although a class or caste system existed in Laredo, most of the townspeople probably did not have any expectations of owning slaves, had never heard of abolitionists, and did not understand the economic and political rivalry between the North and the South. Most likely they could not distinguish between Southerners and Yankees among *americanos*. Yet voters in Laredo and other Rio Grande towns cast their ballots for secession, and the town leaders in Laredo organized companies of *vaqueros* to ride the chaparral in search of Unionists.[2]

Mexicanos on the Border

Crucial to Laredo's participation in the Civil War was the leadership of the Benavides family. Originally from Revilla, the family

---

[1] Ernest Wallace, *Texas in Turmoil*, pp. 42–45, 48–52, 56–62; Seymour V. Connor, *Texas: A History*, pp. 182–85.

[2] Jerry Don Thompson, *Vaqueros in Blue and Grey*, p. 11.

had moved to Laredo during the period of expansion at the turn of the century. One of the sons, José María, married into the Sánchez family and rose to the rank of captain in the Mexican army. Another, Basilio, managed the family's sheep and cattle ranch during the prosperous 1850s and represented the family's interest on the *cabildo*. Don Basilio, *alcalde* at the time of Laredo's endorsement of Canales's efforts to create the Republic of the Rio Grande, fought with other Laredoans, including his nephew, Santos, for the Federalist cause. Don Basilio was also mayor in the last days of Mexican rule and served two terms during the early American period. He was elected county judge in the late fifties and was Webb County's representative in the state legislature when secession became a critical issue in 1859. Without hesitation, don Basilio sided with the faction that favored leaving the Union.[3]

While don Basilio was active in county and state politics, don Santos and his brother, don Refugio, participated in city government. In the elections in December, 1859, the Benavides family, backed in part by some merchants of European extraction, had attempted to take control from the faction led by don Cayetano de la Garza and the *americanos*. When the challengers failed, they contested the results in a local court which ruled in their favor. A new election in January, 1860, resulted in a temporary victory for the Benavides group, but a higher court subsequently reinstated the winners of the first election. The challengers returned, however, and won control in the elections for the 1861 term. The conflict between the two groups continued, but the Benavides faction remained at the helm until 1866, when the full effects of Reconstruction were felt along the Rio Grande.[4]

Mexicano reaction to the Civil War in other parts of South Texas ranged from half-hearted support for the Confederacy to

[3]"The Benavides Family," in John Salmon Ford papers, Texas State Archives, Austin.

[4]See entries for 13, 21, and 22 December 1859, 6, 14, and 27 January, 2, 25, and 28 June, 17 July, 3 October, and 11 December 1860, 8 April, 14 May, 29 June, and 1 December 1861, and 23 August 1862, all in Minute Book, II, City records, Laredo. See also 9, 19, and 26 December 1862, 2 January, 4 April 1863, 5 September 1864, 17 April 1865, and 28 October and 7 and 28 December, 1866, Minute Book, I, and 15 May 1867 and 25 July 1867, Minute Book, A, City records, Laredo.

organized opposition to it. Mexican Americans in Rio Grande City joined a Confederate company under Refugio Benavides, and others in Eagle Pass volunteered for a company in San Antonio, but the countryside near both border towns was never totally secure for the Confederates. Mexican Americans in El Paso extended little support to the southern cause. In the lower Rio Grande Valley an entire Confederate company of *mexicanos* under Adrian J. Vidal switched their allegiance to the Union in the fall of 1863 and threatened to attack Brownsville. Anti-Confederate sentiment and activities by Vidal and others along the Rio Grande were fomented by Unionists who recruited Mexicans and Mexican Americans on both sides of the river and directed guerrilla attacks aimed at disrupting Confederate trade with Mexico. Raids by *enganchados*—those contracted by Union agents—were especially vigorous when directed against the Anglo-Americans who disrupted the established, Hispanic social order along the Rio Grande.

Although some units of Confederates and *enganchados* fought bravely, the allegiance of Mexicans and Mexican Americans to North and South often was questioned because of the high number of desertions. Since the principal goals of the Civil War among the *americanos* were not fully understood by settlers along the Rio Grande, it is not surprising that many *mexicanos* left their units. Furthermore, frequently the men did not receive the supplies and pay promised by the recruiters, and in some cases men left their units in desperation. At times they returned home for planting, harvesting, or the roundup or on account of family obligations.[5]

Anti-*americano* sentiment related to the Civil War first appeared in the spring of 1861 in Zapata County, not far from Laredo. *Mexicanos* there, responding to the leadership of Confederate Henry Redmond, had voted for secession, but the endorsement concealed a deep resentment against Redmond's economic and political control of the county. Redmond, an im-

[5] A. Buchel to Samuel Boyer Davis, 5 December 1861, *The War of the Rebellion: A Compilation of the Official Records of the Union and Confederate Armies*, series 1, IV, 152; Américo Paredes, "Ballads of the Lower Border" (Master's thesis, University of Texas at Austin, 1953), pp. 178–79. See also Thompson, *Vaqueros*, pp. 71–74, 81–83.

migrant from England who had settled in the area shortly after
the Mexican War, had carved out a sizable ranch and had taken
over the political reins of the county by working with *mexicano*
leaders such as Judge Isidoro Vela. When, after the plebiscite of
1861, most Mexican Americans refused to support the southern
cause and "pronounced" against Redmond, Vela, and the Confederate state government, a company of Texas Rangers under
Mat Nolan was sent to quell the uprising.[6]

Nolan captured and executed nine of the leaders of the insurrection but failed to crush the revolt. Mexicans and Mexican
Americans met across the river in Guerrero and planned to seize
the government offices in Carrizo, the county seat, and Redmond's ranch. They were led by Juan Nepomuceno Cortina,
who had remained in the area after he had been defeated by the
U.S. Army in 1859. Informed of the plot, Captain Santos Benavides organized a Ranger company among Laredoans and rushed
to Zapata County to defend the Confederate leaders. But Cortina's forces attacked Redmond's ranch sooner than expected
and, catching the Rangers off guard, forced them to barricade
themselves in the ranch house. When a stalemate developed,
Cortina left a small contingent at the ranch and began preparations to take the courthouse and customs collector's office in Carrizo. A Ranger escaped, however, and sounded the alarm in
Laredo, whereupon don Basilio and his men hurried to Carrizo.
There he routed Cortina before proceeding to Redmond's ranch
to rescue the Rangers. In spite of the victory, don Basilio remained dissatisfied because the battle had been won without
any assistance from Zapata County residents.[7]

Other military activities directed by the Benavideses included patrolling a two-hundred-mile area north and south of
Laredo in search of *enganchados* and bandits. In Camargo, across
from Rio Grande City, a Unionist company had been recruited

[6] *Corpus Christi Ranchero*, 20 April 1861 (copy in Barker Texas History Center,
University of Texas, Austin); Mat Nolan to John S. Ford, 16 April 1861, Ford papers, Texas
State Archives, Austin.

[7] Thompson, *Vaqueros*, pp. 17–23; *Corpus Christi Ranchero*, 18 May and 1 June
1861 (copies in Barker Texas History Center); Santos Benavides to John S. Ford, 23 May
1861, Ford papers.

by E. J. Davis, former deputy collector of customs and district judge at Laredo, and had been drilling during the fall of 1862. Led by Octaviano Zapata, the pro-Union guerrillas attacked a Confederate wagon train on Christmas Day of that year. Captain Refugio Benavides crossed the river a few days later and struck at Camargo in retaliation. Recruiting by Union agents continued, nonetheless. Other border crossings by the Benavideses followed and stirred controversy, but Texans considered the actions by the Benavideses a solution to the bandit problem.[8]

Attacks by *enganchados* and bandits continued throughout 1863 as the war came closer to Laredo. The threat of a northern capture of Brownsville and a campaign by Confederate officials to curb corruption in the trade with Mexico had directed the cotton trains further west, mostly to Eagle Pass, but also to Laredo and other points along the river. In November of 1863 seizure of Brownsville by northern forces finally came. Once on the river, Union General Nathaniel P. Banks lost no time in dispatching Colonel E. J. Davis and the First Texas Cavalry to capture Confederate cotton held in Rio Grande City. Anticipating this, Santos Benavides, by then a colonel, had moved most of the 2,600 bales there to Mexico and had sent some to Laredo to await later shipment. By the time Davis reached Rio Grande City there was little left for him to take. Disappointed, he returned to Brownsville.[9]

In February of the following year, however, a pro-Union force—two cavalry units—appeared unexpectedly a few miles south of Laredo. Distracted by disturbances stirred by a Unionist at Eagle Pass and by difficulties created by the strongman of northern Mexico, Santiago Vidaurri, Colonel Santos Benavides was caught by surprise. Rising from his sickbed, he organized

[8] *Corpus Christi Ranchero*, 8, 15, and 22 January and 24 December 1863 (copy in Barker Texas History Center); John S. Ford to Santos Benavides, 26, 27, and 29 January 1861, and 28 December 1863, Ford papers; Hamilton P. Bee to Don Albino López, *War of the Rebellion*, series 1, XV, 966–67.

[9] Hamilton P. Bee to Santos Benavides, 9 November 1863, and Santos Benavides to Hamilton P. Bee, 12 November 1863, *War of the Rebellion*, series 1, XXVI(1), 409, and XXVI (2), 398–99; *Corpus Christi Ranchero*, 21 January 1864 (copy in Barker Texas History Center).

men from his brothers' companies and from a unit of irregulars who happened to be in Laredo. He also drafted as many townspeople as he could to defend the five thousand bales of cotton in the plaza awaiting shipment to Mexico. He ordered that the cotton bales and his home be burned in the event Union forces broke into Laredo. Men and women stood on the rooftops in an attempt to catch a glimpse of the battle at the outskirts of town. When Confederate reinforcements marched into the plaza, the onlookers gave such a loud cheer that the Unionists, already in partial retreat, fled from the field believing they were outnumbered.

Northern forces were withdrawn from the Rio Grande altogether later that summer, but the men under Benavides continued patrolling the river until the war ended in 1865. The *mexicano* soldiers then returned to their occupations as *vaqueros* and laborers, and the Benavideses gave their attention to their commercial enterprises.[10]

Townlife during the War

The war upset public order in Laredo. No sooner had the conflict broken out than the Board of Aldermen, alarmed by rumors that "suspicious" men would be arriving in town, authorized the creation of a vigilance committee to maintain law and order. The off-duty behavior of the locally recruited soldiers also posed problems, when the men, with money in their pockets and time on their hands, reveled and gambled. After the issuance of one payroll, for example, a fight that erupted in a gambling house left two soldiers dead and others wounded. On another occasion, the killing of a Confederate soldier who had been merry-making in Nuevo Laredo sparked a bitter confrontation between the leaders of the two Laredos. Only the intervention of Mexican and Confederate higher officials prevented the incident from flaring into armed conflict.[11]

The city budget went into the red as a result of wartime ex-

---

[10] Santos Benavides to John S. Ford, 13 and 25 February 1864, Ford papers.

[11] Resolution of the board of aldermen, 14 May 1861, Minute Book, II, City records, Laredo; John Ford to Santos Benavides, 27 and 29 May 1861, Ford papers.

penses and obligations. Although Fort "Maquintoche" was occupied by the *confederados*, the property reverted to the city. The upkeep of the buildings at the fort, plus expenditures made by the municipality for supplies for the troops, put the city over seven hundred dollars into debt. No funds were available from the ordinary sources of revenue to retire the debt or even to pay the interest. To increase the city's income, the aldermen put public lands, including *ejidos* and former fort property, up for sale. This spurred a round of speculation which had to be curbed, first by requiring the buyers to build or fence within six months, and, shortly afterwards, by ending altogether the sale of some land. By early 1863, the city budget was in the clear, but Laredo's continued assistance to the war effort again put the town in debt a year and a half later. City records do not describe how this money was repaid, but presumably common lands continued to be sold until the debt was settled.[12]

The cotton trade and the military activities in this region of the Rio Grande gave Laredo the appearance of a boom town. The trade employed many muleteers and common laborers and turned local merchants into forwarding agents for hundreds of thousands of dollars' worth of cotton passing through Laredo en route to Mexico and for the return flow of goods and supplies destined for the Confederacy. The troops were poorly paid and inadequately supplied, but military expenditures, nonetheless, increased commercial activities. Immigrants flocked into Laredo in response to needs connected with military activities, such as making and hauling hay, providing food, and carting supplies. The payroll dispensed at Laredo created a market for a variety of goods sold by local merchants.[13]

As elsewhere, the closing days of the war posed the threat of disorder in Laredo. Colonel Benavides instructed his brother, Refugio, to take measures against possible disruptions by the soldiers. The Board of Aldermen also authorized the mayor to

[12] See entries for 8 July, 8, 9, and 25 October 1861, 27 November and 11, 16, 19, and 26 December 1862, 2 January 1863, and 6 September 1864, Minute Book, I, City records, Laredo.

[13] *Corpus Christi Ranchero*, 24 December 1863 (copy in Barker Texas History Center).

hire extra policemen. Perhaps because of these precautions, Laredo was spared any trouble when the military companies disbanded.[14]

The effects of Reconstruction were first felt in Laredo when *alcalde* Salinas and three aldermen were removed from their posts by a military order on July 15, 1866. Samuel M. Jarvis was appointed mayor, and W. W. Arnett, M. Everlin, and Cleofas Garza were appointed aldermen. Not all the members of the Benavides faction were replaced, but control of the board returned to the Americans and the de la Garza faction. There is no evidence, however, that Reconstruction elicited the same resentment in Laredo as elsewhere in Texas. Mayor Jarvis was a Unionist who had been exiled in Mexico. While there, he had married a Mexican woman, and his children bore Spanish first names. His assimilation and acculturation may have lessened the opprobrium of having been a Reconstruction appointee.[15]

Political divisions aside, the principal problems for the Board of Aldermen toward the end of the sixties related to law and order. At that time, the board hired an extra policeman to help maintain order in the various entertainment houses, especially dance halls near the center of town, which had become *molestos y nocivos* (bothersome and unwholesome). The board opted to restrict them to one area and threatened to withhold permits altogether if complaints continued. The appearance of these problems at the end of the decade underlined the changes the town had experienced in the 1860s.[16]

Not all the developments in Laredo during the decade were negative or divisive. Wartime commercial activities and consequent prosperity spurred a number of efforts to create public and private schools. Approximately a dozen teachers and schools were subsidized by the Board of Aldermen at various times during the 1860s, including a school established to teach English

[14] Santos Benavides to John Z. Leyendecker, 16 May 1865, John Z. Leyendecker papers, St. Mary's University of San Antonio; resolution, 18 June 1865, Minute Book, I, City records, Laredo.

[15] See entries for 17 August 1868, 4 January, 9 June, 12 July, and 18 October 1869, 7 April and 29 August 1870, and 27 August 1872, Minute Book, A, City records, Laredo.

[16] See ibid., entries for 27 April and 12 July 1869, and 14 December 1870.

to Laredo youths. Assistance to schools included partial or total payment of salaries, limited expenditures for desks and chairs, purchase of books, and in one instance rent-free space in the *casas consistoriales* (city hall). Schools which depended exclusively on city help, however, must have been short-lived, since retractions of earlier commitments to education were not uncommon. Ursuline Academy, established in 1868, supported by the Catholic Church and by tuition, remained the most prominent educational institution in Laredo for decades.[17]

Laredo in 1870

The prosperity experienced in Laredo during the decade of the sixties produced significant population growth but did not prevent the recurrence of the population turnover which had become characteristic of the town's history. By 1870, Laredo's population had increased from 1,306 to 2,043, at an average annual rate of 4.5 percent, which is relatively high compared with the rate of the previous decade. But in spite of this overall growth, at least 2,697 persons who had been in Laredo in 1860 were not there in 1870. Thus, while population growth was an indication of the attractiveness of Laredo, it obscured the problems suggested by the substantial shifts in population.[18]

Some of the population movement, as reflected by the composition of the Benavides company, began before the outbreak of the Civil War. Although the units were reportedly from Laredo, less than one-fourth of the men who served (nineteen out of eighty-seven) had been in Laredo when the 1860 census was taken. Among those not from Laredo, some were from Nuevo Laredo, and others were probably from the surrounding

[17] See entries for 23 November 1860, 1 January, 2 and 27 February, 7 and 8 May, 29 June, 20 August 1861, and 2 January 1862, ibid., and 10 October 1864 and 7 December 1866, 26 June 1867, 25 May 1868, 23 May, 18 October, and 9 December 1869, ibid., I; and Rogelia O. García, *Laredo, Dolores, Revilla: Three Sister Settlements*, pp. 16–17.

[18] With the exception of the information on the Benavides company (Muster Roll, Benavides Company, 11 January 1861, Texas State Archives, Austin), statistics for this and the following paragraphs are compiled from the censuses of 1860 and 1870, National Archives, Washington, D.C.

ranchos. Half of the eighty-seven were in their midtwenties, and the remainder were in their teens or in their thirties and forties, except one who was fifty-five years of age. Most were *mexicanos*; there were only one Anglo-American and one European. Most of the Mexican Americans were Texas-born. Among the Laredo residents in the Benavides company, only the officers had reported any real estate to the 1860 census enumerator, but a handful of the enlisted men had reported personal estates. Only two of all who served were not related to a nuclear family; most of them, about two-thirds, were heads of families.

Population growth and extensive turnover did not alter significantly the size and types of households and dwellings in Laredo. The variations in the household and dwelling size betwen 1860 and 1870 included a small increase in the proportion of small dwellings and households and a comparable decrease among the larger ones. Changes in the types of households and dwellings were also relatively minor. A small increase occurred in households and dwellings headed by single individuals, and a decrease in households and dwellings headed by a nuclear family or made up of several nuclear families.

While the modifications in household and dwelling structure and size were smaller during the sixties than they had been in previous decades, they were, nonetheless, indicative of the changes taking place in Laredoans' family life. The number of persons living in household units composed of or headed by single families rose from 92 in 1860 to 274 ten years later, and the proportion of single individuals in the entire population jumped from 8 percent to 14.2 percent. The increase in single individuals was accompanied by an increase in the number of childless couples. The proportion of these families in Laredo in 1870 rose from 11 percent of all families in 1860 to 16.1 percent in 1870.

A trend toward the concentration of real estate is discernible from the holdings enumerated in 1870. The proportion of potential owners who reported no holdings was much higher in 1870 (93.7 percent) than in 1860 (75 percent). The fact that the listings in 1870 did not include any person whose property was valued under $100—seventeen persons reported holdings that small in 1860—explains only in part the apparent concentration of real estate. In 1870 only one person reported real estate under $500, and that individual listed a holding valued at $100. Interestingly, the number of persons reporting real estate valued $500 and above resembled that of 1860, but the median size of the holdings increased from $360 in 1860 to nearly $1,000 in 1870. The increase of the median real estate holding, however, may be more apparent than real, since smaller holdings seem to have been excluded.[19]

Perhaps because of Laredo's growth, its involvement in state politics, and the immigration of Anglo-Americans, occupations related to government, public service, and the professions engaged a slightly larger proportion of Laredoans in 1870 than in 1860. A rise in the proportion of teamsters among the Laredo work force suggests an increase in the volume of trade, while a decline in the proportion of merchants points to some concentration of business. Perhaps because of the increased trade in clothing, the proportion of Laredoans occupied as tailors and seamstresses had declined by 1870. Changes in rural occupations between 1860 and 1870 also reflect Laredo's growth. The proportion of farmers and graziers declined, while rural laborers increased, indicating a concentration of grazing activities as well as an expansion of them.

The census of 1870 does not reveal any significant improvement in literacy over 1860. Approximately three-fourths of adult Laredoans were still classified as illiterate in 1870. A small number of adults reported that they could read but not write. Both school attendance and literacy were reported for children six to seventeen years, with the expected result that literacy was proportionately higher among those attending school (three-fourths) than among those not attending (one-sixth). The children who had not attended school during the year but who could read and write may have been instructed by their parents, al-

---

[19] Unexplainably, the trend toward concentration of wealth is not clearly evident in the reported personal estates.

though, given the low rate of adult literacy, it is more likely that they had previously attended one of the schools opened during the 1860s.

By 1870 a limited blending of ethnic groups was very evident in Laredo. Perhaps the small number of Europeans and Anglo-Americans in the town made social mixing and intermarriage with the *mexicano* population inevitable. Of thirty-four adult European immigrants in Laredo, six were married and three of the wives were Mexican Americans. Among Anglo-Americans, eight were married to Mexican Americans and one to a European immigrant. From these marriages had sprung twenty-eight children, whose presence helped blur ethnic divisions in the town.

Immigrants from Mexico formed another group in Laredo —one which, in spite of its size, was not as visible as the smaller groups of Americans and Europeans. The 773 Mexico-born Laredoans composed 37.9 percent of the town's population. A little less than a third of them were single individuals apparently not related to a family, whereas only 12.5 percent of the Texas-born *mexicanos* were outside nuclear families. Among the Mexico-born, couples without children constituted 16.7 percent of the nuclear families, 6.5 percent more than that among Texas-born Mexican Americans. Children among the Mexico-born composed a much lower percentage of the entire group (25.7) than among the Texas-born (55.1), although the average family size was about the same. The proportion of single-parent families among the Mexico-born (18.9 percent) was considerably smaller than that among the Texas-born *mexicanos* (30.7 percent).

The relative position of the Mexico-born and the Texas-born in occupational status and in holdings of personal estate and real estate was somewhat ambiguous. Proportionate to all occupations reported by their respective groups, Mexico-born Laredoans reported more unskilled laborers (38.6 percent) and shepherds (16.7 percent) and fewer *vaqueros* (8.6 percent) than did the Texas-born (unskilled laborers, 25.9 percent; shepherds, 2.5 percent; and *vaqueros*, 13.7 percent). Yet the Mexico-born held proportionately twice as many skilled and semiskilled positions (20.7 percent) as did the Texas-born (11 percent). Regarding real estate, the mean value reported by the two groups did not differ significantly: Mexico-born, $1,535; Texas-born, $1,356. But in mean values of personal estates, the difference was rather considerable and in favor of the Texas-born: Mexico-born, $610; Texas-born, $1,129.

Perhaps reflecting their generally low occupational and propertied status in Mexico, Mexico-born Laredoans were appreciably more illiterate than the Texas-born (87.6 percent compared with 78.1 percent), and because of their circumstances in Laredo, only half as many of the children of the Mexico-born attended school as children of the Texas-born. Undoubtedly, Mexican immigrants came to Laredo to improve their economic position, and they may well have done so, but if the ability to send their children to school is an indication of how they fared, their lot in Laredo was not as good as that of the Texas-born Mexican Americans.

The high occupational status and relative wealth of Europeans and Anglo-Americans in Laredo remained very evident. Among the Europeans reporting occupations, two were priests, eight were nuns, five were merchants, four held professional and governmental positions, one was a stock grazier, and the others were employed in crafts and semiskilled jobs. Among the twelve Anglos reporting occupations, six were employed in professional and governmental positions, one was a merchant, one was a sheep grazier, three were in crafts and skilled jobs, and one was employed in an unskilled occupation.

By 1870, Europeans and, to a greater extent, Anglo-Americans had lost some of their preeminence in wealth. In 1860 these two groups combined possessed almost 17 percent of all reported real estate holdings, while in 1870 they held only 13 percent. Also, in 1870, Europeans and Anglo-Americans reported only 25 percent of all the personal property, 10 percent less than in 1860. Holdings reported by Europeans dropped from 22.1 to 20.5 percent; those reported by Anglo-Americans from 13.1 to 4.9 percent. Individual Europeans and Anglo-Americans were still very important in Laredo, however. An Anglo-American, Mayor Jarvis, who reported $5,000 in real estate, was among the three wealthiest landowners in town, and two Europeans, Charles Callaghan and Raymond Martin, reported the top holdings of personal property, $21,000 and $21,475, respectively, and were the wealthiest individuals in Laredo. Political and economic events related to the Civil War had obviously improved the lot of some *mexicanos* in Laredo.

CHAPTER 6

Borderlands in Transition

In their search for wealth, status, and security amidst the turbulent changes of the 1700s and 1800s, settlers in all borderlands communities were subject to the same forces Laredoans faced: prosperity and depression, Indian raids, internal and external warfare, and shifts in population. Even before the events connected with the Mexican independence movement and the subsequent turmoil reached the far northern frontier, residents of San Antonio, Nacogdoches, Santa Fe, Albuquerque, San Diego, Santa Barbara, and Laredo underwent economic expansion and contraction that disturbed the established order in those various communities, affecting the size and permanence of their population; internal racial, ethnic, and social divisions; and the very autonomy of the towns. When Anglo-Americans arrived in the borderlands in the early nineteenth century, townspeople from the Rio Grande to the Pacific endured separation from the fatherland and encountered new and different economic, political, and social forces. Thus, the winds of change that gusted through Laredo after the mid-1700s were the same that swept across the Spanish-Mexican frontier, and settlers in all northern towns reacted and adjusted to developments in broadly comparable, though not always identical, ways.

Settlers and Sojourners

During its early years Laredo exhibited brisk, steady population growth. This was slowed somewhat by the partition of lands in 1767, but immigrants continued to be attracted by the vast unpopulated area beyond the assigned tracts, and Laredo's population rose to about 600 by 1789. As the town extended itself, however, its very prosperity invited intensified raids by Comanches and reportedly by Apaches in the last quarter of the eighteenth century. When insurgents and filibusters in Texas disrupted the Spanish colonial order in 1810, and towns along the Rio Grande less dependent than Laredo on the royal army joined the rebels in the fight for independence, Spanish troops were called away from Laredo, leaving the area open to Indian attack. The Indian menace and other troubles reduced the town's population growth considerably between 1789 and 1819. Nonetheless by this latter date Laredoans numbered 1,418.

Laredo's development in the early 1800s, as in the late eighteenth century, hinged largely on events outside the town and far from the Rio Grande. During the last years of the War of Independence, between 1819 and 1823, population in Laredo ceased to grow and fell slightly. When the garrison returned to Laredo at the war's end, the town experienced a spell of peace and prosperity. A new source of wealth, sheep grazing, appeared in the mid-twenties and spurred a sizable increase in the number of Laredoans, bringing the town population to slightly over 2,000 in 1828. But there was a limit to the expansion which the town and its immediate surroundings could support, and by 1831 Laredo's population had fallen rapidly as the *ranchos* increased in the hinterlands. This expansion, however, invited Indian raids. Perhaps as a result of a return of settlers from the far outskirts to the safety of the town, Laredo's population increased once again between 1831 and 1835, bringing the total number of residents close to that of 1828.

After 1835 the town's economy suffered greatly, and the population declined further. Neglected while the Mexican government struggled with the Texas question, Laredo endured a new wave of Indian raids and, in the midst of this perennial problem, was attacked on different occasions by Texans, Federalists, and Centralists. Finally, in 1846, a few months after the beginning of the Mexican War, Laredo was occupied by a company of American volunteers. After the war the lands and townsite of Laredo were divided in half by the new international boundary of the Rio Grande, and by 1850 its population had plummeted to 1,173. Uncertain of what the new order had in store for them, a significant portion of Laredo's residents had moved to the west bank. The exodus of others, however, had not been motivated by fear. The presence of the American army had brought peace to Laredo and the surrounding area, and the old pattern of moving to the *ranchos* in time of prosperity surfaced once again.

Until the 1860s Laredo experienced neither the spirited growth of its early years nor the prosperity of the twenties. There were changes in the fifties, but the town's prosperity and population growth continued to depend largely on whether or not it received adequate protection against Indian raids. Reduction of the force at Fort McIntosh in the late fifties occasioned the same type of economic recession and reduced growth that Laredo had experienced periodically in the Spanish and Mexican periods. But the military and economic activities of the sixties revitalized Laredo, and its population increased from 1,306 in 1860 to 2,046 in 1870.

Laredo population growth in the eighteenth century was energetic in comparison with that of other borderlands towns. But these early gains in Laredo may have represented only the novelty of expanding opportunities. After the initial spurt, the growth rate was reduced significantly, to the point that it resembled the demographic development of settlements in nearby Texas. For example, San Antonio, established as a *presidio* in 1718 and as a town in 1731, had a population of 1,351 in 1777. Thereafter, the number of inhabitants rose to 1,530 in 1791 before dropping to 1,321 in 1793. The same phenomenon occurred in La Bahía del Espíritu Santo: after rising to 515 in 1777 from its founding in 1721, the population total reached only 728 in 1793. The situation was similar in Nacogdoches: 1777, 347; 1791, 570; and 1793, 457.[1] Since Laredo was founded much later than these Texas settlements, it did not reach its period of stagnation in population growth until after 1789.

Despite New Mexico's earlier settlement, that province's Spanish and caste population remained small. By 1746–48 the population of Santa Fe had reached only 1,800; Santa Cruz and surrounding ranches, 1,560; El Paso del Norte and ranches, 1,080; Albuquerque, 670; Valencia-Tome, 215; and others com-

---

[1] Alicia V. Tjarks, "Comparative Demographic Analysis of Texas, 1777–1793," *Southwestern Historical Quarterly* 77 (January, 1974): table 1.

bined, 419. Forty-two years later, in the census of 1790, none of the large towns had increased in population, and the increase of the entire province was relatively insignificant, from 5,180 to 5,385. In California the growth of Los Angeles from 1781 (21 inhabitants) to 1800 (139) amounted to less than 1 percent average annual growth.[2]

No set pattern of population growth is evident in towns across the borderlands during the Mexican period. The size of Laredo's population peaked in 1828 (2,053 inhabitants), and declined thereafter. San Antonio's population grew to 1,955 by 1819. Unfortunately, census records after that date are unavailable. Population in Los Angeles climbed from 139 in the Spanish period (1800) to 962 in 1830 and 2,550 in 1844. Growth was apparently slower in Santa Barbara; its population had reached only approximately 600 in 1834.[3]

Growth in the American period depended largely on whether or not a particular town was linked to the American economy by the railroad. From 1850 to 1880 Laredo's population rose slowly from 1,173 to 3,811 at the average annual rates of 1.1, 4.5, and 6.4 percent in the intervening decades. But between 1880 and 1890 the number of inhabitants reached 11,319, increasing at the average annual rate of 11.5 percent. That decade the number of inhabitants in San Antonio almost doubled; in Los Angeles the number quadrupled. Other borderlands towns not affected by the railroad expansion during this period did not grow as dramatically until later.

Caste and Wealth

In spite of rapid population growth and economic development in the early formative years, Laredo was a rather harmonious

[2] Alicia V. Tjarks, "Demographic, Ethnic and Occupational Structure of New Mexico, 1790," *The Americas* 35 (July, 1978): tables 1 and 2; Richard Griswald del Castillo, *The Los Angeles Barrio, 1850–1890: A Social History*, pp. 5–6.

[3] Census of 1819, Bexar Archives, in Carmela Leal, "Translation of Statistical Census Reports of Texas, 1782–1836 and Sources Documenting Blacks in Texas, 1603–1803," microfilm, Institute of Texan Cultures, San Antonio; Griswald del Castillo, *Los Angeles Barrio*, pp. 6, 8; Albert Michael Camarillo, *Chicanos in a Changing Society: From Mexican Pueblos to American Barrios in Santa Barbara and Southern California, 1848–1930*, p. 9.

community. Differences among the first two immigrant groups, the early settlers from Dolores and the later ones from Revilla, were resolved as families intermarried and common economic goals were attained. Population and economic growth brought new problems, such as the control of the *corrida*, or roundup, of wild livestock and the maintenance of moral standards, but the leaders of the community worked together toward their solution. After initial difficulties, the captain of the *presidio*, the *cura*, and the *alcalde* avoided open conflicts in carrying out their respective duties.

Two broad opposing currents, however, would eventually curb Laredo's prosperity and pull the community apart. One current generated growth and lured into Laredo immigrants from various social, economic, and racial backgrounds; the other curtailed growth and accentuated differences among the townspeople. The channel for these two currents had been set in the early years when the settlement was on the verge of becoming don Tomás Sánchez's *hacienda*. The *visita* of 1767 modified the *hacienda*-like economic and social structure by allotting lands to all newcomers. Factions vied for domination as a result of the land partitions, but prosperity, immigration, and a new consolidation of power temporarily disrupted the social order. As unrestricted growth became impossible, however, racial and economic distinctions hardened. The landed group, both the first settlers and the early immigrants in the 1750s and 1760s, remained secure, while those who settled in Laredo in the late 1700s either left or accepted less than the promise prosperous times had offered them.

Social and caste distinctions continued to divide Laredoans through the Mexican period and reached into the American era. Censuses before 1824 had classed the people officially as *españoles* and *castas*, Indian, *mestizos*, and *mulatos*, and sometimes accorded upper-class *españoles* the title of *don*. During the period of the republic, the census returns no longer included these distinctions, but their exclusion from the final tabulations was a mere formality. The unofficial drafts of the census of 1835 proved that Laredoans continued to make distinctions of castes and status informally. As late as 1846, the enumerators taking the census ordered by Mirabeau B. Lamar were careful to designate the *dons* and *doñas* within the population. Anglo-Americans in the fifties and sixties often distinguished between the general Mexican populace and "the better elements among the Mexicans" in Laredo.

Wealth distinctions, first seen in the early days when Laredo resembled an *hacienda*, persisted into the 1860s. The existence of peonage, though not its extent, was evident as late as 1846. The renditions of rural properties in 1833 reveal that land-ownership was restricted to a few Laredoans. Occupational and wealth designations in the censuses of 1850, 1860, and 1870 indicate that the divisions between rich and poor continued into the American period and that proportionately fewer Laredoans were in the upper strata of the town's economic and social life in the 1860s than in the 1850s.

The oft-noticed expansion and contraction of the town's population, governed in part by the Indian problem, may have contributed to the perpetuation of the class structure. While some of those moving out of the town during the intervals of stability and prosperity were *rancheros* who were establishing or developing landholdings in the hinterlands, a vast majority of those who migrated in and out of Laredo were probably poor. The constant flow of people through the town prevented the formation of substantial permanent opposition to the landowners. The new commercial wealth of the American period only accentuated class divisions, as is evidenced by the large numbers of unskilled laborers and propertyless Laredoans and by the subordinate position of Mexico-born residents.

Distinctions of race and caste were not peculiar to Laredo. In San Antonio, for example, bias against *mulatos* was very evident, and changes in racial and ethnic classifications were not uncommon, implying extensive racial prejudice. Actual discrimination or segregation is difficult to determine, however, and other factors suggest a considerable amount of tolerance. *Mestizos* and *mulatos* were counted among the owners of ranches, farms, and cattle. Marriage records cite instances of intermarriage among Spaniards and the *castas*, although the extent of intermarriage among San Antonians is difficult to determine given the absence of complete information. Significant proportions of marriages in New Mexico towns were among parties of different ethnic and racial backgrounds: Albuquerque, 29.8 percent; Santa Fe, 28.4 percent; San Juan, 18.3 percent; and Picuris, 26.4 percent. But these marriages occurred mostly among Spaniards and *mestizos* and may have involved lower-class Spaniards who themselves may have been reclassified *mestizos*. Intermarriage among other combinations were few, indicating that racial lines were clearly drawn among most groups in New Mexico.[4]

Along the borderlands race and ethnicity were often intertwined with wealth and status. It was not uncommon for *mestizos* or even *mulatos* who achieved upper-class status to reclassify themselves as *españoles*. Don Antonio Gil Ybarbo of Nacogdoches, perhaps a *mulato*, was listed as Spaniard because of his prominent position in that town and in the province of Texas. In California the wealthy *rancheros* of mixed blood became, after the secularization of the missions, the *españoles* who were later romanticized. Even among this group there were class distinctions, however. Some Spaniards, such as Ybarbo, used the title of *don*.[5] The precise criterion for its usage is difficult to determine. Definitely only *españoles* used the *don*, and in all probability only the wealthy. Perhaps it was also related to seniority in a community. In any case, it appears to have been used with discretion.

Class distinctions were founded on landownership. Before the secularization of the missions and the distribution of the lands, California society exhibited few class distinctions. Likewise, Laredoans enjoyed a more or less even distribution of the available resources before the land allotment of 1767. In San Antonio the few families that made up the settlement outside the Presidio de Béxar found themselves challenged by the Canary Islanders, who arrived with land grants and titles. Across the northern frontier, later waves of immigrants did not acquire land as easily as the first and consequently found themselves in lower economic and social positions.[6]

Settlers in the borderlands did not invent these distinctions

---

[4]Tjarks, "Texas," pp. 322–26; Tjarks, "New Mexico," pp. 72–74, 79–80.

[5]Tjarks, "Texas," p. 326; Griswald del Castillo, *Los Angeles Barrio*, pp. 10–12.

[6]Griswald del Castillo, *Los Angeles Barrio*, p. 11. For San Antonio see Fray Juan Agustín Morfi, *History of Texas, 1673–1779*, ed. Carlos Eduardo Castañeda, II, 293; and Max L. Moorhead, *The Presidio, Bastion of the Spanish Borderlands*, pp. 240–42.

of caste and wealth; they merely reestablished them locally. Apparently many moved up socially and economically either by relocating to the frontier, as did don Tomás Sánchez and the Canary Islanders, or advanced once they were there, as did don Gil Ybarbo, the Benavideses, and others. Such social climbing may even have been easier in the borderlands than in the interior, since in the frontier expansion was often easier. Still, there were many on the frontier for whom landownership and the acquisition of personal wealth were beyond reach. These came and went, mere sojourners in the various borderlands towns.

Ethnic Divisions

At first the American invasion did not seem to affect Laredo adversely. Indeed, the town welcomed the protection against raiding Indians provided by the army. Because the occupation was probably conceived as temporary, town leaders treated Mirabeau B. Lamar and the Americans quite sociably and cooperated in maintaining order. But when it became clear that Laredo would be severed from Mexico, local interests were jeopardized and the initial friendliness ended.

Events in the late forties and early fifties seemed to justify the fears experienced during the transition from Mexican to American rule. The Texas legislature may have calmed anxieties among Mexicans in Laredo by recognizing Spanish land titles, but validation of land titles was also important to the Anglo-Americans who had gone to Laredo with capital, had experience in business, and had commercial ties to distributors of manufactured goods in the United States. They were in a position to buy land at prices which seemed inexpensive to them and excellent to the sellers. Because of the abundance of land around Laredo and the perennial lack of currency, the *mexicano* sellers were probably little concerned over selling parcels to the newcomers. Clear title secured the purchases made by the American and European immigrants, and they soon acquired sizable landholdings.

Although Anglo-Americans and Europeans constituted only

a small fraction of Laredo's population from 1850 to 1870 (never more than 4 percent), they dominated the higher levels of the occupational structure and controlled a disproportionate amount of real estate and personal wealth. As early as 1850 non–Mexican Americans had acquired over 10 percent of the real estate reported by all Laredoans. A decade later they held even greater portions of the real estate (Anglo-Americans, one-tenth; Europeans, one-sixth). They also reported sizable personal holdings (Anglo-Americans, one-eighth; Europeans, one-fifth). *Mexicanos* still held most of the wealth, but were clearly losing ground.

Anglo-Americans also gained control of county government, leaving municipal political offices—the traditional Spanish-Mexican locus of power—in the hands of Mexican Americans. The division of offices was, however, more a cordial and symbolic arrangement than a real distribution of power. Mexican-American leadership of the Board of Aldermen was important as a sign of the continuation of the previous order. The high visibility of aldermen in city government assured property owners, artisans, and laborers that little had changed and that Laredoans need not concern themselves with any power struggle. Yet in the early fifties the merchants, most of them Anglo-American, were firmly in control of city government despite their almost complete absence from elective municipal office. Ordinances on law and order guarded businesses from rowdy behavior by residents and transients. Taxes on stores, while apparently unfavorable to business, were directed against small stores (*vendimias*) which sprouted daily in increasing numbers and were largely Mexican. City improvements made at the request of the merchants benefited commercial properties. With these advantages secured, there was little need for Anglo-Americans to insist on a show of elective power within the town. The arrangement worked well, helping prevent in Laredo a revolt similar to Cortina's in Brownsville.

A revolt of sorts was underway nonetheless. In 1860 the political faction allied with the *americanos* was challenged and thrown out of municipal office by the Benavides family, backed in part by the European merchants. The challengers were successful because American control had never been as complete in

Laredo as it had been in Brownsville. In the first place, Anglo-Americans in Laredo did not have the experience of having dominated the trade in the community nor were they, as in Brownsville, the founders of the town with a clear advantage from the very beginning. Furthermore, in Laredo, Anglo mercantile interests were not as overpowering as they were in Brownsville, and the market was shared with European immigrants who had even greater advantages than did the Americans. Grazing interests also continued to be very important in Laredo, and the old families could not be dislodged easily. Finally, Anglo-Americans of Laredo, though less arrogant than those in Brownsville in their attitude toward the Mexican population, must still have borne the onus of having arrived with the invading force and becoming the lords of the new order.

The conflict over leadership may have contributed to the town's enthusiastic support of the Confederacy. Class consciousness among the elites, a preference for states' rights, political ties with secessionist state leaders, and the perennial concern with defense no doubt influenced the decision to side with the South, but these issues do not fully explain Laredo's vigorous participation in the war. Personal interests and the power struggle within Laredo also played an important part. The war offered the Benavideses a means to extend their influence and control. Through their leadership of the Confederate effort in Laredo, the Benavideses provided defense against Indians and bandits, employed men who might have been out of work, were probably able to secure favors for merchants who were their political allies, and in general, posed a threat to opponents. Overall, they acquired much prestige locally and statewide.

During the decade of the Civil War, *mexicanos* also regained some control over the land and personal property. Their portion of all real estate holdings rose from 73 percent in 1860 to 77 percent in 1870, and their holdings of personal property went from 64 to 74 percent of all such wealth reported. Gains made by Mexican Americans in 1870 were mostly to the disadvantage of Anglo-Americans.

The Europeans, who had backed the Benavides faction, had risen in Laredo's society quickly but quietly. Mostly Frenchmen, they seem to have blended culturally with the *mexicanos* more readily than did the Americans. *Americanos* intermarried with *mexicanos*, but not as early and, quite possibly, not as well as did the Europeans. French priests and nuns probably eased the transition of the church from Mexican to American control and helped consolidate the social position of the Europeans, most of whom were merchants, within the *mexicano* upper class. The church school educated the children of the Europeans and the *mexicano* elites. Church-centered social relationships may have led to intermarriage, economic partnership, and political alliances.

At the other end of the economic scale from the American, European, and Mexican elites were the Mexican immigrants. In wealth and occupational status, they ranked clearly below Texas-born Mexican Americans. Very little else seems to have distinguished them from the Texas-born in Laredo, since the Rio Grande was not a significant barrier to cultural and social bonds and, as newcomers to the east bank, they were following the migration pattern established by the parents and grandparents of the Texas-born *mexicanos*.

In some towns in California the *mexicano* experience was similar to that undergone by Mexican Americans in Laredo; in others, where *mexicanos* were quickly overwhelmed by newcomers, conflicts like the one in Brownsville broke out. In Santa Barbara, Anglo-Americans and Europeans quickly gained numerical and economic prominence after the Mexican War. By 1860 they constituted a third of the town's 2,351 inhabitants. They became wealthy ranchers, professionals, and merchants, and they entered farming, white-collar, skilled, and unskilled occupations. In almost every occupational category their average holdings of real and personal property were greater than the property holdings of *mexicanos* in equivalent occupations. By 1870 the non-*mexicano* population had increased in number and proportionately to the entire population (54 percent) and had accumulated considerably more property than a decade before, surpassing *mexicano* property owners in every occupational category.

Their sudden rise to prominence but not control in the

1850s and early 1860s resulted in frustrations, which found expression in the local paper, the *Santa Barbara Gazette*. The editor, Charles E. Huse, accused the *rancheros* of being against progress because they were unwilling to change to American business enterprises, educate their children in English, and abandon their religious traditions. Huse urged his readers to join the vigilante reprisals against lower-class *mexicanos* who violated the law, especially men like Pío Pico who operated with his band in northern Santa Barbara County. Huse was also upset with *mexicano* control of city government, labeling it as "bad city politics." When the Anglo-Americans finally took control in the early 1870s, the winners viewed their victory as a triumph against backwardness and retrenchment.[7]

In Los Angeles the decline in the number of Mexican Americans who owned land was precipitous. Sixty-one percent of Mexican-American heads of households reported real estate holdings in 1850, 29 percent in 1860, and about 25 percent in 1870. By the time of the latter census the total value of the *mexicano* landholdings had been reduced to about half that of 1850. Properties changed hands quite often as hard-pressed Mexican Americans sold out to Anglo-Americans and to other Mexican Americans.

Changes in the occupations of Mexican Americans in this thirty-year period are misleading. About the same proportion of *mexicanos* in Los Angeles that had been ranchers before the Mexican War continued in that occupation after 1848, but the ratio of professionals, skilled workers, and merchants increased while that of manual laborers decreased. This improvement reflects only the diversification of the economy, and in relationship to the entire community, the proportion of Mexican Americans in upper- and middle-class positions actually declined.[8]

Isolation of Mexican Americans from the economic, social, and political mainstream of Los Angeles resulted in a decade of violence in the post–Mexican War years. In the short period between 1854 and 1870, forty legal executions and thirty-seven

---

[7]Camarillo, *Chicanos in a Changing Society*, pp. 18–25, 29–32, 46–52.
[8]Griswald del Castillo, *Los Angeles Barrio*, pp. 46–57.

lynchings were carried out by Anglo-American town officials and citizenry. Most court trials were travesties of justice, and vigilante violence often took place openly with the implied consent of the authorities. City ordinances restricted or banned traditional amusements, and county officials systematically excluded *mexicanos* from juries. As a reaction to such anti-*mexicano* attitudes and discrimination, some Mexican Americans considered repatriation. Others formed ethnic organizations, countered attacks in newspapers, and encouraged political participation. The rapid growth of the Anglo-American population reduced the impact of these activities, however, and Mexican Americans in Los Angeles lost whatever clout the reorganizational efforts had gained them.[9]

In the new order after 1848, Mexican Americans in Laredo and in California towns faced similar yet different circumstances. The *mexicano* settlement in Laredo was somewhat older than those in California, and the Laredo upper classes were better established. The *ricos* (wealthy) in California apparently had greater wealth than their well-to-do counterparts in Laredo, but had achieved their position of wealth and power only a few years before the American takeover. By contrast, Laredo's landed class already had weathered several decades of turmoil and perhaps were better equipped to deal with the challenges presented by the newcomers from the United States and Europe. Although these differences were important, the crucial factors were time of arrival and the size and strength of the new immigrant group. Anglo-Americans arrived in Nacogdoches, San Antonio, Santa Fe, and many California towns before the borderlands were severed from Mexico. The newcomers to these communities came in larger numbers and with greater capital resources than those who settled in Laredo, and consequently they overwhelmed *mexicano* society in those towns sooner than in South Texas. When Anglo-Americans settled on the Rio Grande frontier in similar proportions, first in Brownsville, and later in Laredo, the results were very similar to those in California.

[9]Ibid., pp. 105–106, 115–20, 125–27, 135–37.

Family Unity

Despite the frontier character of Laredo, membership in a nuclear family was the principal characteristic shared by most townspeople, from Laredo's foundation up to 1789. But problems related to population growth in the late eighteenth century destroyed this harmony. Crowded housing made privacy difficult to obtain. The lack of wells and sources of water other than the river gave rise to problems of decency associated with bathing. The increase in population resulted in greater anonymity among Laredoans than before, and unacceptable behavior could no longer be controlled through personal admonition. As private moral concerns became public issues, Laredoans resorted to city ordinances in order to preserve the integrity of the nuclear family.

The problem lay not merely with the increase in the population but also with its turnover. Migrants flowed into the town during the prosperous years when the troops provided defense for the town and its environs. Recurring crises—insurrection, civil wars, invasion, Indian threats—sent settlers fleeing from Laredo, and the temporary resolution of these crises brought them back. Even prosperity posed problems, since expansion placed greater responsibilities on the undermanned and ill-equipped *presidiarios*. Thus throughout the 1800s, the absence of long, undisturbed periods of slow but steady growth characteristic of the earlier period affected family life adversely, as the large number of "widows" and the high rates of illegitimacy imply.

Surprisingly, some abatement of the forces which were destroying family unity appeared during the decade of the Civil War, a period as disruptive for Laredo as those preceding it in the nineteenth century. The census of 1870 records an increase in the proportion of two-parent families. This reversal in the trend set in the censuses of 1850 and 1860 can be explained in part by the fact that the Confederate unit formed in Laredo and stationed there furnished a good amount of protection against the real or feared Indian threats.

Shifts in Laredo's male-female ratios exemplify the upheaval caused by the migrations in and out of the towns, but such sexual imbalance was not unique to Laredo. In 1789 Laredo's population exhibited a relatively stable sexual balance of 105 males for every 100 females. By comparison, the Texas censuses of 1777 and 1793 recorded ratios mostly between 114 and 125 to 100. The same high ratios were evident in Spanish and Mexican Nacogdoches. Likewise, the New Mexican census of 1790 listed an average ratio of 110 to 100. This ratio excludes that for Santa Fe, where an unusual number of servants, widows, and unmarried women heads of households changed the trend of male dominance prevalent elsewhere. In Santa Fe there were 88 males per 100 females.[10] Similar circumstances existed in Laredo in 1819, when the ratio of males plummeted to 84, indicating the population shifts which resulted from the changing conditions along the Rio Grande during the Mexican War of Independence. The ratios of males to females aged eight to sixteen years, young adults aged seventeen to twenty-five years, and mature persons aged twenty-six to forty years, fell even more in the remaining year before the Constitution of 1824.

Likewise, the appearance of census "widows" was not peculiar to Laredo; Spanish censuses for Texas and New Mexico reveal the same phenomenon. The situation in Laredo, as depicted by the wartime census of 1819 and others, was more critical, however. While in the Texas and New Mexico census widows composed only between 1 and 10 percent of the entire adult population, widows in Laredo in 1819 accounted for 13 percent. Also, while in Texas and New Mexico, the sex ratios for both the entire population and for the combined group of the widowed and the unmarried were male-dominant, in Laredo in 1819 the sex ratios were female-dominant for both (69 males for every 100 females).[11] Further study of wartime and Mexican censuses for Texas and New Mexico may reveal that population growth, the struggle for independence, and the transition into the national

[10]Tjarks, "Texas," pp. 304–306, and "New Mexico," pp. 62–63; James M. McReynolds, "Family Life in a Borderlands Community: Nacogdoches, Texas, 1779–1861" (Ph.D. diss., Texas Tech University), p. 117.

[11]Tjarks, "Texas," pp. 310–13, and "New Mexico," pp. 67–69; McReynolds, "Family Life in a Borderlands Community," appendix table 1.

period produced similar turmoil in the sex ratios and increased the number of widows.

Authorities in towns other than Laredo were also faced with scandalous conduct related to sexual morality. In Nacogdoches the presence of large numbers of unmarried soldiers, slaves, and transients was in part responsible for the prostitution of the town wives, causing worried authorities to threaten severe punishment. Similar problems existed in Los Angeles, according to some reports. In Texas, church records reveal an illegitimacy rate of 20 percent in 1799.[12] In Laredo the illegitimacy rates in the years before the War of Independence averaged 14 percent, but this rose gradually until 1818; then it zoomed to 26.9 percent in 1818 and to 45.1 percent in 1823. Undoubtedly ecclesiastical insistence on sacramental marriage coupled with the lack of priests to administer it and the absence of strong church-related traditions among some groups explains high rates of illegitimacy. Still, the presence of troops and the increase and shifts of the population account for much of the disruption of traditional family life.

Related to the problems of widows and illegitimacy were the high percentages of one-parent families. In Laredo these made up only about one-twentieth of all nuclear families in 1789, then increased to about 25 percent in 1819, and to 33 percent in 1850 and 1860. The census of 1870 reveals a slight reduction (down to 25 percent). In Texas, one-parent families jumped from 22 and 20 percent in San Antonio and La Bahía in 1779–80 to 32 and 31 percent in 1790. In New Mexico the percentage of one-parent families in 1790 ranged from 22 to 36 in the various towns.[13] High mortality among men may explain this, but only in part. Abandonment and illegitimacy were also the causes of these high rates.

While the percentage of households headed by single individuals in Laredo and Los Angeles increased throughout the American period, the composition of the nuclear family house-

[12] McReynolds, "Family Life in a Borderlands Community," pp. 143–45; Tjarks, "Texas," pp. 313–17. Also see David J. Weber, "Mexico's Far Northern Frontier: Historiography Askew," *Western Historical Quarterly* 7 (July, 1976): 292.

[13] Tjarks, "Texas," pp. 319–20, and "New Mexico," pp. 77–78.

holds was changing. In Laredo the percentage of households made up of extended nuclear families rose slightly, from 18 percent of all households in 1850 to 23 percent in 1860 and 1870, while in Los Angeles the percentages dropped from 70 in 1844 and 1850 to a range between 40 and 50 percent in the following three decades. The decline in California may reflect the turmoil ushered in by migrations there, while the increase in Laredo suggests the expansion of the family to improve its resources.

Nuclear families headed 96 percent of all households in Laredo in 1850, but by 1860 and 1870 this figure fell to 81 and 79 percent, respectively. A similar decline in households headed by nuclear families was experienced in Los Angeles: from approximately 90 percent in 1844 and 1850 to 76, 78, and 80 percent in the following three censuses. This latter trend corresponds to the percentage of households with nuclear families in Nacogdoches during the years 1779 to 1860.[14] The declines correlate with the increasing number of unmarried and unrelated immigrants into the borderlands communities following the American acquisition of the Southwest.

Family life in Laredo was similar to that in other borderlands communities. Males predominated among adults; illegitimacy, if not widespread, was not uncommon; one-parent families composed a significant portion of all nuclear families; the number of widows was much greater than that of widowers; and authorities often used their office to preserve public morality. Serious as these problems were, especially since they were nonexistent in the early years of settlement, they do not appear to have reached alarming proportions in any of the communities except Laredo, and this did not occur until the turmoil of the War of Independence and subsequent political conflicts ushered in rapid population growth and turnover. By 1870, once life in Laredo became more settled and secure, a reversal in the deterioration of the traditional nuclear family was evident. In the remaining decades of the nineteenth century Laredo's population grew more dramatically than ever before, but only further study

---

[14] Griswald del Castillo, *Los Angeles Barrio*, pp. 98–100. Also see McReynolds, "Family Life in a Borderlands Community," pp. 167–68.

can reveal whether the changes in those years created the same kind of crisis in family life that the earlier events produced.

Autonomy and Dependence

Laredo began as a settlement independent of government assistance. The founders did the preliminary scouting themselves, furnished all the supplies for the expedition, and provided the necessary defense for the fledgling settlement. But after 1767, when population increased and expanded to the hinterland, Laredoans could no longer furnish their own protection and became increasingly dependent on the viceregal government of New Spain for military assistance. After 1824 this reliance was transferred to the Mexican Conservatives, whose policies included a strong central government which offered Laredoans hope of obtaining an efficient presidial force. When the Conservatives failed to provide such a force and Laredo sank into serious depression, the town leaders switched their allegiance to the Federalists. As things turned out, however, the Federalists offered even less by way of defense than the Centralists had.

Adequacy of defense made the difference in Laredo between growth and loss of population, stability and instability, prosperity and depression. The degree of protection also influenced indirectly the formation of the town's class structure and the extent of family unity among Laredoans. The inadequacy of the presidial force at Laredo ultimately left the town open to attack and invasion by Texans and Americans. The townspeople, seemingly passive and helpless, were at the mercy of outside forces.

Laredoans in the 1840s and 1850s faced a new threat in the form of Anglo-American economic and political domination. The reaction of the *mexicano* elites to the incipient power struggle with the newcomers from the United States is open to various interpretations. Given the fact that county government demanded greater acquaintance with a law and polity strange to them, they may have chosen more or less consciously to cede control of the county and to entrench themselves in the town through their dominance of the Board of Aldermen. The upper-class Mexican Americans, whose economic interests were nearer to those of the *americanos* than to those of the *mexicano* lower classes, made a political compromise not based on ethnicity but rather on economic realities and potential. Still, the political events of the sixties seem to indicate a persistent intent among the inner circles of Laredo's well-to-do to quietly prevent the kind of takeover by *americanos* experienced in other southwestern communities.

Yet the fortunes of all Laredoans, Mexican American, Anglo-American, and European immigrant alike, remained largely outside their control. The reduction of the forces at Fort McIntosh toward the end of the 1850s occasioned the same type of recession which the withdrawal of the *presidio* had caused in earlier days. Ingeniously as Laredoans adapted to the intricate ethnic patterns of the town and enterprising as the new merchants seemed in comparison with the *comerciantes* (small itinerant or resident merchants) of the preceding periods, economic crises still occurred and could be solved only by means which Laredoans themselves could not provide.

Despite the confluence and partial success of the forces pitted against Laredo and the fact that outsiders sometimes judged the townspeople to be indolent and complacent provincials, Laredoans did attempt to overcome considerable geographical limitations and external pressures. During the Spanish and Mexican periods the strides in education, the beginning of local merchandising, the efforts to counter raiding Indians, the decision to endorse different political movements and counter-revolutions, the shift in the grazing economy from cattle to sheep, and even the flight of peons from the oppressive debt system reflected the efforts of Laredoans to control their own destiny. In the 1850s, Laredoans appeared overwhelmed as they continued to face the familiar problems of defense, caste and wealth divisions, and family disunity in addition to adjusting to changes introduced by Anglo-American and European merchants, churchmen, and officials. The Civil War, however, seems to have provided *mexicanos* an opportunity to display their own self-reliance. Through leadership and participation in the war, Laredoans defended themselves and introduced stability and order that allowed them to hold on to their place in the chaparral. War, depression, invasion, and internal division had not pried them from their toehold on the Rio Grande.

Mexican Americans in California faced even greater changes in their communities after 1848 than did Laredoans. Rapid population increase and turnover in Los Angeles, for example, undermined the political base of *californio* elites. Still, the initial setback did not constitute a continual steady loss of power, and *mexicanos* retained control of half of the county posts and of various city offices. A precipitous decline did occur after 1880, when large numbers of Anglo-American newcomers altered the ethnic balance of the city's population. Not surprisingly, only those *californios* whose families had assimilated with Anglo-Americans through marriage, business, or friendships participated in politics.[15]

In Santa Barbara the deterioration of *mexicano* control came sooner than in Los Angeles. In the 1850s and early 1860s Santa Barbara was the stronghold of Mexican-American political power in southern California, but by the late 1860s racial partisan politics, gerrymandering, exclusion from political parties, and harassment worked together to eliminate Mexican participation. In San Salvador the creation and eventual separation of Anglo-American Riverside preserved Mexican-American political control in the old town, but excluded *mexicanos* from the economic development of the wider community. Elsewhere, such as in San Diego, the decline in the political power of Mexican Americans was swifter than in the other *mexicano* towns.[16]

Loss of political power was attributable mostly to the economic and demographic changes in the various towns. To be sure, political strategy played an important role, but the rapid and overwhelming increase of Anglo-Americans with skills, capital, and business connections was the principal reason for the loss of *mexicano* political power. In some California towns this occurred soon after 1848; in others it did not take place until after 1880. Laredo's experience was similar, save that *mexicano*

[15]Griswald del Castillo, *Los Angeles Barrio*, pp. 153–60.
[16]Camarillo, *Chicanos in a Changing Society*, pp. 109–13.

involvement in the Civil War slowed down Anglo-American encroachment into city politics. Still, Mexican politicians in Laredo were unable to withstand the demographic and economic pressures which accompanied the new wave of immigrants that came to Laredo after the railroad reached that Rio Grande town.

Epilogue

The cattle industry boom which swept the state in the post–Civil War period and the disorder and violence which accompanied it reached the Rio Grande in the 1870s. Horses and cattle from the area had been driven to Louisiana since Spanish and Mexican times, but their numbers had never been large because the market was limited. In the Texan and American periods the market increased somewhat, but the expansion of the farming frontier prevented large drives to Louisiana. The extension of the railroad into Kansas and the removal of most of the Indians from South and West Texas by the army after the Civil War facilitated unprecedented expansion in the cattle industry. Enterprising merchants and companies with their own capital or financed by foreign investors acquired large landholdings. These ranching empires sprang up next to the settled frontier, where small farmers at times only barely managed to make a living. The lure of rapid wealth attracted individuals from these areas and distant places who were willing to pursue violence to get rich quick. The pattern of violence had already been set by some big ranchers, who maintained virtual standing armies and used them along with capital and entrepreneurship to expand their holdings. Ironically, the vastness of their lands made raiding by the bandits easier.[17]

Although both Anglo-Americans and *mexicanos* availed themselves of the unattended flocks, many of the Anglo-American outlaws became folk heroes while the Mexican *vaqueros* were labeled *bandidos*. Mexican raiders were especially hated because they enjoyed a sanctuary across the Rio Grande, al-

[17] Sandra L. Myres, *The Ranch in Spanish Texas, 1691–1800*, pp. 43–50; Seymour V. Connor, *Texas, A History*, pp. 254–57.

though there is no conclusive evidence that *mexicanos* stole more cattle than their Anglo-American counterparts. The *bandido* epithet appears to have been hurled principally by law-enforcement officers and those they represented, namely, the merchants and the new ranchers. It may be that these individuals were covering their own guilt over the violence and theft that accompanied their takeover of South Texas. The American public went along with the view of the Mexican as thief because it had already adopted a pejorative image of the *mexicano*.[18]

The conviction that most Mexicans were thieves justified the widespread retaliation that was visited upon *mexicanos* on both sides of the Rio Grande. The greatest perpetrators of this violence were the Texas Rangers, who set out to create a reign of terror along the border in order to stop the raids. Ranger L. H. McNelly created a reputation by displaying the slain bodies of alleged *bandidos* in the main square in Brownsville and by crossing the border to attack bandit sanctuaries. On one occasion McNelly stormed a supposed bandit hideout below the Rio Grande, killing four men and frightening women and children. It turned out to have been the wrong *ranchería*. In Laredo, B. D. Lindsay and six other Rangers without provocation attacked a party of *vaqueros*. The *mexicanos* returned the Rangers' fire from behind their fallen horses until the local sheriff, who happened on the scene, explained to the Rangers that the supposed *bandidos* were two of Laredo's leading citizens. The Rangers' only explanation was that had the *vaqueros* been bandits and the Rangers not fired first, they (the Rangers) would surely have been killed.[19]

Responsibility for controlling the bandit problem also fell on Mexican officials. Anxious not to incur the disfavor of the U.S. government, whose recognition they sought, both Benito Juárez and Porfirio Díaz reinforced army contingents along the

[18] Américo Paredes, *With A Pistol in His Hand*, pp. 15–23. Also see David J. Weber, *Foreigners in Their Native Land*, pp. 59–61, and Weber, *New Spain's Far Northern Frontier: Essays on Spain in the American West*, pp. 295–304.

[19] Walter Prescott Webb, *The Texas Rangers*, pp. 264–65; George C. Pierce, *A Brief History of the Lower Rio Grande Valley*, pp. 110–11.

border to prevent the harboring of Texas cattle south of the Rio Grande as well as to stop the raiding of Mexican cattle which were being driven to U.S. markets. Although Mexican action on this issue was never as swift as the Americans had hoped for, the presence of Mexican *rurales* (a quasi-military force) became the key to pacifying the border region.[20]

Help in ending the bandit troubles also came from some leading Mexican Americans. In 1874 Refugio Benavides formed a regiment of the state police in Laredo to assist in controlling the border ruffians. Benavides's outfit also crossed the Rio Grande to avenge thefts on the Texas side and to apprehend rustlers fleeing into Mexico. His efforts are often credited with sparing the Laredo area from banditry.[21] While Benavides's actions do appear forceful, it is questionable whether Laredo was threatened with as much banditry as other areas along the Rio Grande. Following the pattern set during the Civil War, Benavides was utilizing the regiment not only to capture outlaws but also to regain and secure for his family and the old *ranchero* faction the political power lost during Reconstruction. In this manner local autonomy was restored, at least temporarily.

The most significant change for Laredo in the post-Reconstruction period came not from the increase in cattle and the raiding but from the arrival into town of the railroad. Almost unexpectedly Laredo became the meeting point for four railroads: the Texas-Mexican from Corpus Christi; the International and Great Northern, a national system which connected Laredo with San Antonio and Saint Louis; the Ferrocarriles Nacionales de México, an American-built railroad system reaching into Central Mexico, which formed part of Porfirio Díaz's modernization program; and the Rio Grande and Eagle Pass, which joined Laredo with northern Mexico. Both the Texas-Mexican and the Mexican National reached the border in November of 1881, and immediately trade which once flowed through Matamoros and Brownsville began to be diverted through Laredo and Corpus

[20] J. Fred Rippy, *The United States and Mexico*, pp. 282–95.
[21] J. B. Wilkinson, *Laredo and the Rio Grande Frontier*, pp. 351–52.

Christi. Uriah Lott, the merchant and banker from Corpus Christi who had launched the railroad to Laredo, and ranchers Richard King and Mifflin Kenedy, who rescued the investment, came to Laredo by special car in early December as part of the inauguration activities. Later that month Laredo celebrated the arrival of the International and Great Northern with the visit of army notables and their spouses. The following year the Rio Grande and Eagle Pass entered Laredo.[22]

With the arrival of the railroads, merchandising took on greater importance than before in Laredo's economy, and Anglo-Americans who arrived with capital and business connections gained political influence. The new merchants formed the Citizens party and soon began to challenge the control held by the Democratic party, whose power had been restored after Reconstruction. The very name of the Citizens party reflected Anglo-American domination within that faction, though the party also counted some prominent Europeans who had broken with Benavides and other *mexicano* elites who ruled the Democratic party. Because the Citizens party represented the interests of the new upper class, its members were commonly referred to as Las Botas, the well-heeled or boot-wearers. Democrats were called Los Huaraches, those who wore Mexican poor-man's sandals. Despite their formal and informal names, party lines cut across economic and ethnic barriers. Personal loyalties made for unlikely combinations, and personal and family feuds created political enemies out of former fellow party members. Nevertheless, the rise of the new party in the mid-1880s indicated a definite shift of political power from the established *mexicano* elites to the newly arrived Anglo-American merchants and their recently won European allies.

In the 1886 spring elections Las Botas, the new party, made an almost clean sweep of city and county offices. Jubilant, Las Botas staged a mock funeral of Los Huaraches. As the Bota procession carrying a casket symbolic of their defeated opponents reached the main plaza, it was met by a sizable force of mounted,

[22] Ibid., pp. 362–66.

armed Huaraches, who opened fire on the entourage. The "mourners" hit the ground, scattered, and shot back. The battle continued for about half an hour until army troops from Fort McIntosh restored order. The riot left an estimated twenty-five dead and forty wounded. State troops arrived within a few days, but by that time all trouble had disappeared.

Suspiciously, the Botas were not caught entirely unprepared and may well have wanted, if not actually planned, the shoot-out. The election returns a few days before had actually sealed the fate of Los Huaraches. Thereafter the old *mexicano* elites settled for a minor role in a bipartisan coalition called the Independent Club. Formed at the turn of the century, this party dominated local politics until the 1970s.[23]

As elsewhere, the introduction of the railroads into Laredo brought about significant change. Even before the final miles of track were laid, the town's population had risen from 2,043 in 1870 to 3,521 in 1880. By 1890 it soared to 11,319, and continued to increase, to 13,429 in 1900 and 14,855 in 1910. Other changes were also evident. The Laredo Improvement Company was formed in the 1880s and was instrumental in the development of the Heights as well as other new sections of town. In the 1890s small coal deposits were discovered not far from Laredo, irrigation facilitated the creation of many truck farms, and a steel bridge replaced the ferry, making commerce with Mexico easier. Electric trains brought residents from across the creek into downtown. The *escuela amarilla* (the yellow schoolhouse) was rebuilt into Old Central. Other schools were opened, requiring the hiring of a school superintendent.[24]

In the process of rapid growth Laredo developed into two societies, one Anglo-American and one Mexican-American. The Anglo-American was depicted in the pages of the *Laredo Times*. Founded in 1881, the *Times* boasted of the town's energetic growth, reported the activities of the various social clubs and

[23] Wilkinson deemphasizes the Anglo versus Mexican interpretation of the political divisions (Ibid., pp. 370–72).

[24] *Texas Almanac and State Industrial Guide, 1982–1983*, p. 190; Seb S. Wilcox, "Webb County," pp. 4–8, in Laredo Archives, St. Mary's University of San Antonio.

the church-related schools, and kept Laredoans abreast of state and national news. Anglo-American members of the local Lodge of the Improved Order of Red Men, one of the many brotherhoods in Laredo, began the Washington's Birthday celebration in 1897 as their counterpart to the Dieciseis (Mexican Independence Day) festivities.[25] Anglo-Americans could not remain completely apart, however, and some limited social mixing and intermarriage did take place among the upper classes of all three cultural groups. According to local tradition, from this and from daily interaction with the large Mexican population, some Anglo-Americans became Mexicanized.

With all the changes, Laredo's Mexican-American society was taking on a new character. New waves of Mexicans and Mexican Americans from across the Rio Grande and from other parts of Texas also entered Laredo. These new immigrants did not have any personal ties or loyalties to the old *ranchero* class. Some of them had been educated in Mexico and had been exposed to revolutionary political ideas. Highly politicized, they edited a number of Spanish-language small newspapers: *La Crónica, El Horizonte, El Defensor del Obrero,* and *El Demócrata Fronterizo.* In 1911, Nicasio Idar, one of these editors, called together *mexicano* leaders from across the state to protest violence perpetrated against Mexican Americans by law enforcement officers. Participants in the Primer Congreso Mexicanista reaffirmed their Mexican-American identity, called for better schools, and demanded an end to the violence. Although the Congreso failed to establish a permanent organization, other groups, brotherhoods, mutual aid societies, and small, neighborhood private schools sponsored cultural activities and provided a variety of community services at the turn of the century.[26]

Despite the protests of the participants in the Congreso, violence reached new heights in South Texas in that decade. The year before the Congreso met, Mexican exiles in San Antonio,

[25] Seb S. Wilcox, "The Story of Washington's Birthday Celebration of Laredo," p. 3, in Laredo Archives.

[26] José E. Limón, "El Primer Congreso Mexicanista de 1911: A Precursor to Contemporary Chicanismo," *Aztlán* 5 (Spring and Fall, 1974): 85–117.

Eagle Pass, Del Rio, and Laredo had launched a revolution from their Texas bases against Mexican President Porfirio Díaz. The chaos of the revolution pushed more immigrants into the newly developed agricultural regions in South Texas. Conflicts between them and the new entrepreneurs from the Midwest broke out as the spirit of revolution and revolutionaries themselves crossed the Rio Grande. A plan was devised in San Diego, Texas, not far from Laredo, calling for a revolt against Anglo-American landowners and the eventual separation of the Southwest from the United States. Raids followed, and the Texas Rangers reacted with vengeance, slaying perhaps as many as 5,000 Mexican Americans along the Rio Grande.[27]

Spared from all the violence, Laredo's population soared in the early twentieth century, even throughout the Great Depression. The townspeople stood on the rooftops to witness some battles of the Mexican Revolution fought across the river in Nuevo Laredo, and the raids and Ranger killings were far to the south in the Valley. Laredo's population jumped from 14,855 in 1910 to 22,710 in 1920, 32,618 in 1930, and 39,274 in 1940. With the onset of the depression, immigrants from other parts of the Southwest returned to Mexico, and some may have settled in Laredo. Caravans of repatriates crossing through Laredo became quite common as the depression worsened. Some of the returnees were penniless and, according to local tradition, bakers, grocers, and other charitable Laredoans assisted them on their journey home.

The outbreak of World War II opened a new chapter in the history of Laredo and South Texas. Prosperity returned, and so did new immigrants. By 1950, Laredo's population had risen to 51,694.[28] Prosperity also created a wider tax base for schools and municipal improvements. Returning Mexican-American veterans had acquired new experiences and participated vigorously in social and political activities. Since the fifties, Laredo has changed dramatically because of an Air Force base established in the previous decade, the expansion of trade with Mexico, and

---

[27] Paredes, *With a Pistol in His Hand*, p. 26; Webb, *Texas Rangers*, pp. 484–86.
[28] *Texas Almanac, 1982–1983*, p. 190.

new wealth in gas and oil. As in prerailroad days, divisions based on wealth, ethnicity, length of residence, and social position (established and new families, old and new money) persist, but, as before, unity and cooperation also exist, as residents, Laredoans all, find ways of making a living and obtaining security and status in this hot and dusty chaparral region.

Appendix

TABLE 1

Population and Average Annual Rate of Change, Laredo, 1757–1870

Census Year	Population	Intercensal Average Annual Rate of Change
1757	85	
1767	185	8.8
1789	597[a]	5.5
1795	636	[b]
1819	1,418	2.3
1820	1,417	[b]
1823	1,402	[b]
1824	1,570	12.0
1828	2,053	7.0
1831	1,698	−6.5
1833	1,746	1.4
1835	1,979	3.9
1837	1,736	−3.2
1845	1,884	1.0
1846	1,891	[b]
1850	1,173	[c]
1860	1,306	1.1
1870	2,043	4.5

SOURCES: Laredo Archives, St. Mary's University of San Antonio; Gulick and others, *Papers of Lamar*, IV(1), 44–65; Calleja report, in Vigness, "Nuevo Santander in 1795"; censuses of 1850, 1860, 1870, National Archives, Washington, D.C.

[a] Does not include 111 Indians.

[b] Insignificant change.

[c] Loss due mainly to new international boundary.

TABLE 2

Ethnicity, Marital Status, Sex, and Seniority, Laredo Population, 1789

	Adults				Children				Total Popula- tion
	Married		Single						
Ethnicity	M	F	M	F	M	F	Males	Females	
Spaniard	63	63	60	55	41	39	164	157	321
Mulato	31	28	30	26	18	22	79	76	155
Mestizo	23	25	21	22	16	14	60	61	121
Indian	18	18	15	20	25	25	58	63	111
TOTAL	135	134	126	123	100	100	361	357	718

SOURCE: Laredo Archives, St. Mary's University of San Antonio.

TABLE 3

Sex and Seniority,
Laredo Population, 1795

Seniority	Male	Female	Total
Adults	188	196	384
Children	148	104	252
TOTAL	336	300	636

SOURCE: Calleja report, in Vigness, "Nuevo Santander in 1795."

TABLE 4

Ratios Spanish to Non-Spanish, by Age and Sex, Laredo, 1819, 1820

Years of Age	Spanish Males: Non-Spanish Males		Spanish Females: Non-Spanish Females		Spanish Total: Non-Spanish Total	
	1819	1820	1819	1820	1819	1820
0–7	79:108	113:83	75:92	111:84	154:200	224:167
8–16	61:88	37:23	68:86	82:48	129:174	119:71
17–25	47:48	49:30	51:54	93:21	98:102	142:51
26–40	54:69	56:39	70:95	85:84	124:164	141:123
41–50	27:44	74:72	28:45	46:57	55:89	120:129
51 and over	30:29	48:48	30:40	18:16	60:69	66:64
TOTAL	298:386	377:295	322:412	435:310	620:798	812:605

SOURCE: See table 2.

TABLE 5

Age and Sex Distribution by Marital Status,
Laredo, Various Years, 1819–37

	1819		1820		1823		1824		1828		1831		1835		1837	
	Male	Female	Male	Female	Male	Female	Male	Female	Male	Female	Male	Female	Male	Female	Male	Female
Single[a]																
0–7	187	167	196	196	207	215	153	124	231	336	191	188	256	277	298	304
8–16	149	154	58	129	64	142	177	179	200	180	147	141	208	207	97	133
17–25	79	62	77	78	84	96	93	91	183	113	118	110	112	39	100	132
26–40	31	22	63	36	22	31	108	101	69	18	97	51	17	4	68	44
41–50	8	1	40	2	33	2	5	2	19	9	6	3	12	2	0	0
51 and over	4	2	11	2	5	2	3	2	5	4	0	0	6	8	0	0
(All single)	(458)	(408)	(446)	(442)	(412)	(488)	(539)	(507)	(707)	(560)	(559)	(493)	(611)	(537)	(563)	(613)
Married[a]																
17–25	16	39	2	34	3	40	0	2	75	84	31	34	55	60	73	106
26–40	90	111	32	107	30	6	116	121	119	137	106	102	225	232	73	58
41–50	58	46	102	62	98	56	55	52	83	72	99	99	62	55	67	12
51 and over	47	20	77	10	70	3	37	33	59	41	30	4	23	4	20	10
(All married)	(211)	(216)	(214)	(214)	(201)	(105)	(208)	(208)	(336)	(334)	(266)	(299)	(365)	(351)	(233)	(186)
Widowed[a]																
17–25	0	4	0	2	0	5	0	0	2	0	0	0	8	20	0	0
26–40	2	32	0	26	0	24	3	25	2	6	2	8	19	18	33	42
41–50	5	26	4	39	3	38	2	20	9	33	4	19	16	24	11	25
51 and over	8	48	8	22	6	19	10	48	11	54	17	61	4	6	12	18
(All widowed)	(15)	(110)	(12)	(89)	(9)	(86)	(15)	(93)	(24)	(93)	(23)	(88)	(47)	(68)	(56)	(85)

SOURCE: See table 2.

[a]Single population includes children; married and widowed population includes those seventeen years of age and over.

TABLE 6
Age and Sex, Laredo Population, 1845[a]

Years of Age	Males	Females	Total
0–7	159	270	429
8–16	230	200	430
17–25	159	171	330
26–40	171	151	322
41–50	136	87	223
51 and over	61	89	150
TOTAL	916	968	1,884

SOURCE: Gulick and others, *Papers of Lamar*, IV (1), 44–65.
[a]The census of 1845 did not provide marital status.

TABLE 7
Wealth Resources, Laredo, Various Years, 1757–1835

Resource	1757	1795	1824	1828	1831	1833	1835
Horses	874	1,832	325	356	2,408	2,400	548
on the range	712	1,239	a	a	a	a	a
tamed	162	593	a	a	a	a	a
Mules	125	368	150	256	280	140	125
Burros	31	68	a	a	a	a	a
Cattle	101	984	2,000	2,673	2,408	3,900	2,548
Sheep and goats	9,080	12,822	700	3,223	6,430	6,500	5,800
Corn (*fanegas*)	a	a	a	122	129	a	60

SOURCES: Laredo Archives, St. Mary's University of San Antonio; Calleja report, in Vigness, "Nuevo Santander in 1795."
[a]Data not given.

TABLE 8
Percent of Family and Household Heads and Independent Adults Reporting
Real Estate, Laredo, 1850, 1860, 1870

Dollar Value of Real Estate	1850 (N=618)	1860 (N=428)	1870 (N=847)
None	83.2	75.0	93.7
50–249	0.5	10.3	0.1
250–499	0.5	3.3	0.0
500–999	6.8	5.8	2.8
1,000–4,999	6.3	4.9	3.0
5,000–9,999	2.2	0.7	0.4
10,000–24,000	0.5	0.0	0.0

SOURCES: U.S. censuses, 1850, 1860, 1870, National Archives, Washington, D.C.

TABLE 9

Percent of Family and Household Heads and Independent Adults Reporting
Personal Estate, Laredo, 1860, 1870[a]

Dollar Value of Personal Estate	1860 (N=428)	1870 (N=847)
None[b]	50.0	69.3
50–249	29.7	15.5
250–499	12.2	9.4
500–999	4.4	1.2
1,000–4,999	2.6	2.9
5,000–9,999	0.9	0.9
10,000–24,000	0.2	0.7

SOURCES: See table 8.

[a] Personal Estates were not reported in the 1850 census.

[b] Thirty-five persons, or 8.2 percent of family and household heads and independent adults, in 1860 reported personal property valued less than $50. In 1870 amounts less than $50 were not recorded.

TABLE 10

Percent of Adult Working Population in Each Occupation, Laredo,
1850, 1860, 1870

Occupation	1850 (N=282)	1860 (N=529)	1870 (N=685)
Public service, professional	2.6	1.5	3.8
Merchant, clerk	2.1	6.0	3.7
Craft, skilled	18.3	12.0	19.5
Semiskilled	2.1	19.6	8.4
Farming, stockgrazing	19.9	6.1	4.4
Unskilled	54.9	54.6	59.1

SOURCES: See table 8.

TABLE 11

Percent of Population by Family Status, Laredo, 1850, 1860, 1870

Family Status	1850 (N=1,173)	1860 (N=1,306)	1870 (N=2,043)
Head of family	22.4	21.2	19.0
Spouse	15.4	13.2	14.3
Offspring	52.5	52.6	46.3
Single	9.7	13.0	20.3

SOURCES: See table 8.

TABLE 12
Percent of Families in Each Family Category, Laredo, 1850, 1860, 1870

Family Category	1850 (N=241)	1860 (N=254)	1870 (N=385)
Childless couple	9.9	11.0	16.1
Couple with children	62.3	56.3	58.2
Single parent with children	27.8	32.7	25.7

SOURCES: See table 8.

TABLE 13
Percent of Households and Dwellings by Household Category, Laredo, 1850, 1860, 1870

Household Category	Households			Dwellings		
	1850 (N=265)	1860 (N=280)	1870 (N=451)	1850 (N=233)	1860 (N=268)	1870 (N=448)
Single individual	2.2	12.5	15.5	0.8	11.9	17.4
Nuclear family	78.1	58.1	54.6	63.9	56.0	51.0
Single individual plus others	1.8	6.1	8.9	1.7	8.6	9.1
Nuclear family plus others	17.7	22.9	21.0	33.5	23.5	22.5

SOURCES: See table 8.

TABLE 14
Percent of Households and Dwellings by Number of Members and Inhabitants, Laredo, 1850, 1860, 1870

Members, Inhabitants	Households/ Dwellings		Households			Dwellings		
	1789 (N=130)[a]	1846 (N=308)[b]	1850 (N=265)	1860 (N=280)	1870 (N=451)	1850 (N=231)	1860 (N=268)	1870 (N=432)
1	3.1	1.3	1.5	9.5	9.5	0.4	9.3	8.6
2–4	50.8	37.3	56.6	41.7	45.9	47.2	40.5	43.8
5–9	44.6	50.6	38.5	43.5	41.5	47.6	43.1	43.3
10 and over	1.4	10.7	3.4	5.0	3.1	4.6	7.1	4.4

SOURCES: See table 8.

[a] Enumeration in the census of 1789 was not made by dwelling.

[b] Households and dwellings were not separated in the census of 1846.

TABLE 15

School Attendance, Children Aged Six through Seventeen Years, by Sex, Laredo, 1850, 1860, 1870

School Attendance	1850		1860		1870	
	Male	Female	Male	Female	Male	Female
Attending	104	82	29	42	43	26
Not attending	98	87	205	188	240	239
TOTAL	202	169	234	230	283	265

SOURCES: See table 8.

TABLE 16

Adult Literacy, by Sex, Laredo, 1850, 1860, 1870

Literacy	1850		1860		1870	
	Male	Female	Male	Female	Male	Female
Can read and write	133	64	201	66	115	45
Cannot write	a	a	13	34	a	a
Cannot read and write	156	186	407	419	213	293
TOTAL	289	250	621	519	328	338

SOURCES: See table 8.

a Not applicable for the 1850 and 1870 censuses.

TABLE 17

Population of Seven Southwest Cities, by Decade, 1850–90

City	1850	1860	1870	1880	1890
Laredo	1,173	1,306	2,043	3,811	11,319
San Antonio	3,487	8,235	12,256	20,550	37,673
Los Angeles	1,610	4,385	8,504	11,183	50,395
Santa Barbara	a	2,351	2,640	3,460	5,864
San Bernardino	a	940	a	1,673	4,012
Santa Fe	a	4,635	4,765	6,635	a
Albuquerque	a	1,203	1,307	a	a

SOURCES: U.S. censuses for 1850, 1860, 1870, 1880, 1890, National Archives, Washington, D.C.

a Data for the municipality are included with data for larger entity such as precinct or county and so are not reported here.

Glossary

alcabala	sales tax
alcalde	mayor
amo	master
arrieros	teamsters
bandido	bandit
bandos	proclamations, decrees
botas	boots; in Laredo (cap.), boot wearers, the party of the rich
cabeceras	district government seat
cabildo	city council
capitán	captain
casa de campo	ranch house
casas consistoriales	city hall
casta	mixed-blood, caste
comerciante	small merchant
compadrazgo	compaternity, relationship between a child's parents and godparents
compañía volante	flying or roving company
conquistador	conqueror
corrida	roundup
cortes	parliament
criollo	Creole; Spaniard born in the New World
cura	curate, parish priest
Dieciseis	September 16, Mexican Independence Day
ejidos	town common
enganchado	Mexican contracted by Union agent (Civil War)
entrada	expedition for conquest or settlement
español	Spaniard, Mexican of Spanish descent or high social rank
expediente	file
fandango	public dance
finca rústica	rural holding
hacendado	head of hacienda

hacienda	large estate
huaraches	sandals; in Laredo (cap.), sandal wearers, the party of the the common people
indios	American Indians
indios agregados	settled Indians attached to Spanish town
indios bárbaros	nomadic Indians
indita	Indian woman; implies youth or low social status
jacal	one-room hut made of sticks and mud, with thatched roof
justicia mayor	chief justice
mestizaje	racial mixture
mestizo	person of mixed Spanish and Mexican ancestry; generally, person of mixed race
milpa	cornfield
molesto	bothersome
mulato	person of mixed black and white ancestry
nocivo	unwholesome
norteño	northerner
padrino	baptismal sponsor
peso	Mexican monetary unit, equal to eight reales
pilón	promotional incentive
piloncillo	dried sugar cane
plaza	town square
porción	portion, land allotment
presidiales	soldiers
presidio	garrison
préstamo forzoso	forced loan
primeros pobladores	town founders, first settlers
ranchería	settlement cluster
ranchero	rancher
rancho	ranch
real	monetary unit, one-eighth of peso
reducción	village of converted Indians
regidor	alderman
Revillano	resident of Revilla
rico	Mexican or Mexican American of the landed class
rodeo	roundup
rurales	quasi-military peacekeeping force
sitio	parcel of common pastureland assigned to an individual

soltero	unmarried adult
sujeto	dependent town
vaquero	cowboy
vendimia	small shop
villa	town
visita	inspection
visitador	inspector

Bibliography

Archival Collections

Austin, Texas. General Land Office. Acta de la Visita de Laredo, 1767.
———. Texas State Archives. John Salmon Ford Papers, 1864–92.
———. University of Texas. Eugene C. Barker Texas History Center. Laredo Archives, 1749–1836. Matamoros Archives, 1811–59.
Laredo, Texas. Office of the City Clerk. City Records, 1848–70.
———. Office of the County Clerk. Records of the Commissioners' Court, 1848–70.
———. Office of the District Clerk. District Court Records, 1848–70. Webb County Records.
———. St. Augustine Catholic Church. Baptismal and Burial Records, 1789–1870. Papers of Rev. Florencio Andrés.
San Antonio, Texas. Office of the County Clerk. Bexar County Archives.
———. St. Mary's University of San Antonio. Laredo Archives, 1767–1853. John Z. Leyendecker Papers, 1863–65. Seb S. Wilcox Papers, c. 1940.
Washington, D.C. Office of the Adjutant General. Post Returns, 1850–59 (microfilm copy).
———. National Archives. Manuscript returns of the United States seventh census (1850), eighth census (1860), ninth census (1870), and tenth census (1880) (microfilm copies).

Government Documents

Estado general de las fundaciones hechas por d. José de Escandón en la Colonia de Nuevo Santander. 2 vols. Mexico City: Talleres Gráficos de la Nación, 1929.
U.S. Congress. House. *House Executive Document,* no. 52. 26th Cong., 1st Sess.
———. House. *House Executive Document,* no. 93. 45th Cong., 1st Sess.
———. Senate. *Congressional Globe,* no. 540. 35th Cong., 1st Sess. 1848.

War of the Rebellion: A Compilation of the Official Records of the Union and Confederate Armies. Four Series, 81 vols., Washington, D.C., 1880–1901.

Works Progress Administration. *Report 420.* San Antonio, Texas, 1938.

Newspapers

American Flag (Brownsville). 1846–47.
El Ancla (Brownsville). 1840.
Corpus Christi Ranchero. 1861–63.
El Mercurio del Puerto de Matamoros. 1836.
Laredo Times. 1881–1910.

Theses, Dissertations, and Papers

Bailey, David Thomas. "Stratification and Ethnic Differentiation in Santa Fe, 1860 and 1870." Ph.D. dissertation, University of Texas at Austin, 1975.

Camarillo, Albert Michael. "The Making of a Chicano Community: A History of Chicanos in Santa Barbara." Ph.D. dissertation, University of California at Los Angeles, 1975.

Graf, LeRoy. "The Economic History of the Lower Rio Grande Valley, 1820–1875." Ph.D. dissertation, Harvard University, 1942.

Irby, James Arthur. "Line on the Rio Grande: War and Trade on the Confederate Frontier, 1861–1865." Ph.D. dissertation, University of Georgia, 1969.

Leal, Carmela. "Translation of Statistical Census Reports of Texas, 1782–1836 and Sources Documenting Blacks in Texas, 1603–1803." Microfilm. Institute of Texan Cultures, San Antonio.

McReynolds, James M. "Family Life in a Borderlands Community: Nacogdoches, Texas, 1779–1861." Ph.D. dissertation, Texas Tech University, 1978.

Paredes, Américo. "Ballads of the Lower Border." Master's thesis, University of Texas at Austin, 1953.

Peter, Robert K. "Texas: Annexation to Secession." Ph.D. dissertation, University of Texas at Austin, 1977.

Riley, John Dennis. "Santos Benavides: His Influence on the Lower Rio Grande, 1823–1891." Ph.D. dissertation, Texas Christian University, 1976.

Tijerina, Andrew A. *"Tejanos* and Texas: Native *Mexicanos* of Texas, 1820–1850." Ph.D. dissertation, University of Texas at Austin, 1977.

Books and Articles

Acuña, Rodolfo. *Occupied America.* New York: Harper & Row, 1972.

Alessio Robles, Vito. *Coahuila y Texas desde la consumación de la independencia hasta el tratado de Guadalupe Hidalgo.* Mexico City: Talleres Gráficos de la Nación, 1945–46.

Almaráz, Félix D. "Governor Antonio Martínez and Mexican Independence in Texas: An Orderly Transition." *Permian Historical Annual* 15 (December, 1975): 44–55.

————. *Tragic Cavalier.* Austin: University of Texas Press, 1971.

Alperovich, M. S. *Historia de Independencia de México.* Translated by Adolfo Sánchez Vázquez. Mexico City: Editorial Grijalbo, 1967.

Archer, Christen I. *The Army in Bourbon Mexico, 1760–1810.* Albuquerque: University of New Mexico Press, 1977.

Audubon, John Woodhouse. *Audubon's Western Journal, 1849–1850.* Cleveland: A. H. Clark, 1906.

Bannon, John Francis. *The Spanish Borderlands Frontier, 1531–1821.* New York: Holt, Rinehart, and Winston, 1970.

————. *Bolton and The Spanish Borderlands.* Norman: University of Oklahoma Press, 1958.

Barclay, George W. *Techniques of Population Analysis.* New York: Wiley, 1958.

Barker, Eugene C. *Mexico and Texas, 1821–1835.* 1928. Reprint. New York: Russell and Russell, 1965.

Benedicto, Luis. *Historia de Nuevo Laredo.* Nuevo Laredo, Tamaulipas, 1956.

Benson, Nettie Lee. *Mexico and the Spanish Cortes, 1810–1822.* Austin: University of Texas Press, 1966.

Berlandier, Luis, and Rafael Chovel. *Diario de viaje de la comisión de límites que puso el gobierno de la república, bajo la dirección del exmo. sr. general de división d. Manuel de Mier y Terán.* Mexico City: Tipografía J. Navarro, 1850.

Billington, Ray Allen. *The Far Western Frontier.* New York: Harper & Row, 1966.

Bogue, Donald J. *Principles of Demography.* New York: Wiley, 1969.

Bolton, Herbert Eugene. *The Spanish Borderlands: A Chronicle of Old Florida and the Southwest.* New Haven: Yale University Press, 1921.

————. "Tienda de Cuervo's *Ynspección* of Laredo, 1757." *Southwestern Historical Quarterly* 6 (January, 1903): 187–203.

Camarillo, Albert Michael. *Chicanos in a Changing Society: From Mexican Pueblos to American Barrios in Santa Barbara and South-*

ern California, 1848–1930. Cambridge, Mass., and London: Cambridge University Press, 1979.

Castañeda, Carlos E. *Our Catholic Heritage in Texas.* 7 vols. Von Boeckmann–Jones, 1936–58.

———, trans. and ed. "*A Trip to Texas in 1828* by José María Sánchez," *Southwestern Historical Quarterly* 29 (April, 1926): 249–88.

Caughey, John W. *Hubert Howe Bancroft, Historian of the West.* New York: Russell and Russell, 1946.

Chevalier, François. *Land and Society in Colonial Mexico.* Berkeley and Los Angeles: University of California Press, 1970.

Connor, Seymour V. *Texas: A History.* Arlington Heights, Illinois: AHM, 1971.

———, and Odie B. Faulk. *North America Divided.* New York: Oxford University Press, 1971.

Curti, Merle E. *The Making of an American Community: A Case Study of Democracy in a Frontier County.* Stanford: Stanford University Press, 1959.

Cutter, Donald. "Dedication to the Memory of Hubert Howe Bancroft." *Arizona and the West* 2 (Summer, 1960): 105–106.

Davis, James Edward. *Frontier America, 1800–1840: A Comparative Analysis of the Settlement Process.* Glendale: Clark, 1977.

Dobyn, Henry F. *Spanish Colonial Tucson: A Demographic History.* Tucson: University of Arizona Press, 1976.

Domenech, E. *Missionary Adventures in Texas and Mexico.* London: Longman, Brown, Green, Longmans, and Roberts, 1858.

Faulk, Odie B. "The Presidio: Fortress or Farce." In Oakah L. Jones, *The Spanish Borderlands.* Los Angeles: Lorrin L. Morrison, 1974.

Folsom, George. *Mexico in 1842.* New York: C. J. Folsom, Wiley and Putnam, Robinson, Pratt, 1842.

García, Rogelia O. *Laredo, Dolores, Revilla: Three Sister Settlements.* Laredo: Privately printed, 1970.

———. *The Song of La Grande Agua.* Austin: Privately printed, 1974.

Garrett, Julia Kathryn. *Green Flag Over Texas.* New York: Pemberton Press, 1939.

Gerhard, Peter. *A Guide to the Historical Geography of New Spain.* Cambridge: Cambridge University Press, 1972.

Gibson, Charles. *Spain in America.* New York: Harper & Row, 1966.

Goldfinch, Charles W. *Juan N. Cortina, 1824–1892: A Re-Appraisal.* Brownsville, Texas: Bishop's Print Shop, 1950.

Gómez-Quiñones, Juan, and Luis Leobardo Arroyo. "On the State of Chicano History: Observations on Its Development, Interpretations, and Theory, 1970–1974." *Western Historical Quarterly* 7 (April, 1976): 155–85.

Góngora, Mario. *Studies in the Colonial History of Spanish America.* Cambridge: Cambridge University Press, 1975.

Green, Thomas J. *Journal of the Texan Expedition Against Mier.* 1845. Reprint. New York: Arno Press, 1973.

Griswald del Castillo, Richard. *The Los Angeles Barrio, 1850–1890: A Social History.* Berkeley and Los Angeles: University of California Press, 1979.

Gulick, Charles Adams, Jr., and Katherine Elliot, eds. *The Papers of Mirabeau Buonaparte Lamar.* 6 vols. Austin: Texas State Library, 1920–27.

Hackett, Charles W. *Pichardo's Treatise on the Limits of Louisiana and Texas.* 4 vols. Austin: University of Texas Press, 1931–46.

Hale, Charles A. *Liberalism in the Age of Mora, 1821–1853,* New Haven and London: Yale University Press, 1968.

Haring, C. H. *The Spanish Empire in America.* New York: Harcourt, Brace, & World, 1947.

Harris, Walter D. *The Growth of Latin American Cities.* Athens: Ohio University Press, 1971.

Hill, Lawrence F. *José de Escandón and the Founding of Nuevo Santander: A Study of Spanish Colonization.* Columbus: University of Ohio Press, 1926.

Hobsbawn, E. J. *Primitive Rebels: Studies in Archaic Forms of Social Movement in the 19th and 20th Centuries.* New York: Norton, 1965.

Horgan, Paul. *Great River: The Rio Grande in North American History.* 2 vols. New York: Rinehart, 1954.

John, Elizabeth A. H. *Storms Brewed in Other Men's Worlds: The Confrontation of Indians, Spanish, and French in the Southwest, 1540–1795.* College Station: Texas A&M Press, 1975.

Jones, Oakah L., Jr. *Los Paisanos: Spanish Settlers on the Northern Frontier of New Spain.* Norman: University of Oklahoma Press, 1979.

Lea, Tom. *The King Ranch.* 2 vols. Boston: Little, Brown, 1957.

Limón, José E. "El Primer Congreso Mexicanista de 1911: A Precursor to Contemporary Chicanismo." *Aztlán* 5 (Spring and Fall, 1974): 85–118.

López, Diego G. *Historia del peso mexicano.* Mexico City: Fondo de Cultura Económica, 1975.

Ludecus, Edward. *Reise durch die Mexikanischen Provinzen Tamau-lipas.* Leipzig: J. F. Hartknoch, 1837.

Luna Rodríguez, Miguel. *Reseña histórico-geográfica de Tamaulipas.* Ciudad Victoria, Tamaulipas: Privately printed, 1957.

Meinig, D. W. *Imperial Texas.* Austin: University of Texas Press, 1969.

———. *Southwest: Three Peoples in Geographical Change.* New York: Oxford University Press, 1971.

Mintz, Sidney W., and Eric R. Wolf. "An Analysis of Ritual Parenthood (*Compadrazgo*)." In Jack M. Potter et al., eds., *Peasant Society: A Reader.* Boston: Little, Brown, 1967.

Moorhead, Max L. *The Apache Frontier.* Norman: University of Oklahoma Press, 1968.

———. *The Presidio: Bastion of the Spanish Borderlands.* Norman: University of Oklahoma Press, 1975.

Morfi, Fray Juan Agustín. *History of Texas, 1673–1779.* Edited by Carlos E. Castañeda. 2 vols. Albuquerque: Quivira Society, 1935.

Mörner, Magnus. *Race Mixture in the History of Latin America.* Boston: Little, Brown, 1967.

Myres, Sandra A. *The Ranch in Spanish Texas, 1691–1800.* El Paso: Texas Western Press, 1969.

Nance, Joseph M. *After San Jacinto: The Texas-Mexican Frontier, 1842.* Austin: University of Texas Press, 1963.

Newcomb, W. W. *The Indians of Texas.* Austin: University of Texas Press, 1961.

Oates, Stephen B., ed. *"Rip" Ford's Texas by John Salmon Ford.* Austin: University of Texas Press, 1963.

Paredes, Américo. *With a Pistol in His Hand.* Austin: University of Texas Press, 1971.

Pierce, George C. *A Brief History of the Lower Rio Grande Valley.* Menasha, Wisconsin: George Banta, 1917.

Powell, Philip Wayne. *Soldiers, Indians and Silver.* Berkeley and Los Angeles: University of California Press, 1952.

Price, Glenn W. *Origins of the War with Mexico.* Austin: University of Texas Press, 1967.

Reeve, Frank D. "A Letter to Clio." *New Mexico Historical Review* 31 (April, 1956): 102–32.

Richer, Juan E. *Reseña histórica de Nuevo Laredo.* Nuevo Laredo, Tamaulipas: Privately printed, 1958.

Rippy, J. Fred. *The United States and Mexico.* New York: F. S. Crofts, 1926.

Robertson, William Spence. *Iturbide of Mexico*. New York: Greenwood, 1968.

Roel, Santiago. *Nuevo León*. Monterrey, Nuevo León: Librería México, 1944.

Sánchez, José María. "A Trip to Texas in 1828." *Southwestern Historical Quarterly* 29 (April, 1926): 249–88.

Schroeder, John H. *Mr. Polk's War*. Madison: University of Wisconsin Press, 1971.

Scott, Florence Johnson. *Historical Heritage of the Lower Rio Grande Valley*. Waco, Texas: Texian Press, 1966.

———. *Royal Land Grants North of the Rio Grande*. Rio Grande City: Distributed La Retama Press, 1969.

Sierra, Justo. *Evolución política del pueblo mexicano*. Mexico City: Casa de España en México, 1940.

Sonnichsen, C. L. *The El Paso Salt War, 1877*. El Paso: Hertzog, 1961.

———. *Pass of the North: Four Centuries on the Rio Grande*. El Paso: Texas Western Press, 1968.

Sosa, Octaviano. "Creación y denominación de la Villa de Nuevo Laredo." In *Centenario de Nuevo Laredo*. San Antonio: Artes Gráficas, 1948.

Spicer, Edward H. *Cycles of Conquest*. Tucson: University of Arizona Press, 1962.

———. *Plural Society in the Southwest*. New York: Arkville, 1972.

Swadesh, Frances Leon. *Los Primeros Pobladores: Hispanic Americans of the Ute Frontier*. Notre Dame, Ind.: University of Notre Dame Press, 1974.

Tate, Bill, ed. *Guadalupe Hidalgo Treaty of Peace, 1848, and the Gadsden Treaty with Mexico, 1853*. Espanola, New Mexico, 1970.

Texas Almanac and State Industrial Guide, 1982–1983. Dallas: A. H. Belo Corporation, 1981.

Thompson, Jerry Don. *Sabers on the Rio Grande*. Austin: Presidial Press, 1974.

———. *Vaqueros in Blue and Grey*. Austin: Presidial Press, 1976.

Tilden, Bryant Parrot. *Notes on the Upper Rio Grande*. Philadelphia: Lindsay & Blakiston, 1847.

Tjarks, Alicia V. "Comparative Demographic Analysis of Texas, 1777–1793." *Southwestern Historical Quarterly* 77 (January, 1974): 291–338.

———. "Demographic, Ethnic and Occupational Structure of New Mexico, 1790." *The Americas* 35 (July, 1978): 45–88.

Vigness, David M., trans. and ed. "Nuevo Santander in 1795: A Provincial Inspection by Félix Calleja." *Southwestern Historical Quarterly* 75 (April, 1972): 461–506.

Wallace, Ernest. *Texas in Turmoil*. Austin: Steck-Vaughn, 1965.

Ward, H. G. *Mexico in 1827*. 2 vols. London: H. Colburn, 1928.

Webb, Walter Prescott. *The Texas Rangers*. 1935. Reprint. Austin: University of Texas Press, 1965.

———, and H. Bailey Carroll, eds. *The Handbook of Texas*. 2 vols. Austin: Texas State Historical Association, 1952.

Weber, David J. *Foreigners in Their Native Land*. Albuquerque: University of New Mexico Press, 1973.

———. "Mexico's Far Northern Frontier: Historiography Askew." *Western Historical Quarterly* 7 (July, 1976): 279–93.

———. *New Spain's Far Northern Frontier: Essays on Spain in the American West*. Albuquerque: University of New Mexico Press, 1979.

Wilcox, Seb S. "Laredo During the Texas Republic." *Southwestern Historical Quarterly* 42 (October, 1938): 83–107.

———. "The Laredo City Elections and the Riot of 1886." *Southwestern Historical Quarterly* 45 (July, 1941): 1–23.

———. "The Spanish Archives of Laredo." *Southwestern Historical Quarterly* 49 (January, 1946): 341–60.

Wilkinson, J. B. *Laredo and the Rio Grande Frontier*. Austin: Jenkins, 1975.

Woodman, Lynn. *Cortina: The Rogue of the Rio Grande*. San Antonio: Naylor, 1951.

Worcester, Donald E. "The Significance of the Spanish Borderlands to the United States." *Western Historical Quarterly* 7 (January, 1976): 5–18.

Wortham, Louis J. *A History of Texas*. 5 vols. Fort Worth: Molyneaux, 1924.

Ximenes, Ben Cuellar. *Gallant Outcasts*. San Antonio: Naylor, 1963.

Zea, Leopoldo. "La ideología liberal y el liberalismo en México." In *El liberalismo y la reforma en México*. Mexico City: Universidad Nacional Autónoma de México, 1957.

Index

www.ingramcontent.com/pod-product-compliance
Lightning Source LLC
Jackson TN
JSHW071133080326
99007JS00020B/352